LOVE'S
LABOR

LOVE'S LABOR

Twenty-five Years of Experience in the Practice of Psychotherapy

STANLEY E. GREBEN, M.D.

Foreword by
Jerome D. Frank, M.D., PH.D.

SCHOCKEN BOOKS • NEW YORK

First published by Schocken Books 1984
10 9 8 7 6 5 4 3 2 1   84 85 86 87
Text copyright © 1984 by Stanley E. Greben
Foreword copyright © 1984 by Schocken Books Inc.
All rights reserved

Library of Congress Cataloging in Publication Data
Greben, Stanley E.
    Love's labor.
    1. Psychotherapy—Addresses, essays, lectures.
I. Title.
RC480.G72 1984   616.89'14   83–040460

Designed by NANCY DALE MULDOON
Manufactured in the United States of America
ISBN 0–8052–3896–4

To my teachers, *with gratitu*

To John Claire Whitehorn
from whom I learned the value of rigorous, hu

To Lewis B. Hill,
*who demonstrated the therapeutic power of unc
insightfulness;*

To Aubrey Lewis,
who showed the merit of impatience with intelle

To Jerome D. Frank,
*who has always had the courage of his someti
convictions; and*

To Olive Cushing Smith,
*with whom I came to understand the simple h
psychoanalysis.*

CONTENTS

FOREWORD

THIS book contains the wisdom distilled from twenty-five years of practice by a thoughtful, psychoanalytically oriented psychotherapist. Trained as a psychoanalyst, Dr. Greben has freed himself from the constricting conceptual and procedural shackles of psychoanalytic orthodoxy, while retaining and developing those features that possess therapeutic power. He has abandoned analytic detachment and passive listening in favor of active involvement. He openly conveys empathic concern, caring, respect, and realistic hopefulness and does not hesitate to take firm charge when necessary or to help the patient to independence when appropriate. At the same time, Dr. Greben retains belief in the special power of self-awareness to enhance the patient's ability to handle the problems that brought him to therapy, and to foster personal growth. Analysis of the transference—the reciprocal feelings of patient and therapist in the treatment situation—retains its place as an important medium of therapeutic change.

For Dr. Greben, psychotherapy is an example of all mutually responsible, close human encounters. The success of a psychotherapeutic enterprise, like that of a marriage, depends on mutual commitment and trust, as well as on the ability of both partners to withstand and profit from disappointments, conflicts, and other sources of pain. Psychotherapy differs essentially from other enduring intimate relationships in that one of the participants, by virtue of special knowledge and experience, brings to it healing or growth-stimulating components.

This view is expressed with exceptional clarity and grace in simple language free of jargon. Points are abundantly illustrated with excerpts from interviews.

Consistent with his conviction that the success of therapy depends heavily on the personal qualities and attitudes of the therapist, Dr. Greben throughout reveals his own thoughts and feelings without embarrassment or defensiveness. Nor does he hesitate to ask his patients to evaluate his therapy, and he accepts their criticism and praise with equal composure. In presenting a revealing self-portrait, Dr. Greben succeeds to a remarkable degree in overcoming the barrier of print, so that he becomes a real person to the reader—a dedicated, perceptive, compassionate therapist, open to his own feelings as well as the patient's and sufficiently secure emotionally to weather and learn from the vicissitudes of the therapeutic encounter.

As an account of long-term, psychoanalytically oriented psychotherapy, this book may be dismissed by some readers as being out of fashion in a field currently dominated by promulgators of short-term, quick-fix approaches; and, indeed, these may be appropriate for many more patients than psychoanalysis has recognized. But there will always be damaged or vulnerable patients who need long-term help.

Moreover, to conclude that because this book comes out of the psychoanalytic tradition, it is of interest only to others with a similar orientation, would be grossly to underestimate its value. While superficially this is a how-to-do-it book, and an exceptionally good one, at a deeper level it is a penetrating inquiry into fundamental aspects of all human relationships. It is an insightful account of the suffering engendered by human predicaments and of the power of hope, empathic understanding, and trust, not merely to alleviate the suffering, but to enable the sufferer to master his predicament and derive strength from it.

Reading *Love's Labor* is an enriching intellectual and emotional experience, not only for beginning and experienced psychotherapists of all persuasions, but for patients as well—in fact, for everyone who seeks to deepen his understanding of himself and his fellow human beings. I venture to predict that its quiet voice will be heeded and appreciated long after the voices of many of its currently fashionable rivals have faded into oblivion.

JEROME D. FRANK, M.D., PH.D.

ACKNOWLEDGMENTS

THE writing of this book has been possible because of much help from the people close to me. My family have provided constructive suggestions, guidance, and encouragement. Close friends have read the work in progress and made valuable and supportive comments.

Bill Freedman gave a helpful evaluation of the first draft.

Harvey Hart guided, criticized, and gave form to the content. Betty Oliphant was of enormous help in editing, improving, and refining both drafts.

Joyce Seltzer helped find the right publisher. The first draft was typed by Daphne Aucock, the second by Blanche Stuart.

The Laidlaw Foundation provided a grant which allowed me the time to write the first draft.

INTRODUCTION

In 1954, having graduated as a physician from the University of Toronto, and having interned at a very large county hospital in Brooklyn, I began residency training in order to become a psychiatrist. In 1958, I began psychiatric practice, and not long thereafter, also became trained as a psychoanalyst.

My training was at excellent institutions, with very good teachers: three years at The Johns Hopkins Hospital in Baltimore, and one year at the Maudsley Hospital in London. My psychoanalytic training took place in Montreal. That training, superimposed upon an education first in physiology and biochemistry, and then in medical school, set the foundation, basically scientific and academic, for my professional work. It prepared me to begin to be a psychiatrist and psychoanalyst. However, it did not prepare me for some surprises which later developed in the course of my work. While much of what I was taught held true, much of it did not. And much of what I learned from my patients and through my own observation and experience, was considerably different from what I had been taught and what I had read.

That discrepancy is the reason I felt a need to put forward my views on what I consider to be most important in the psychotherapeutic experience. I have been in no hurry to reach conclusions, since I believe it requires many years to become competent in any line of work. However, after twenty-five years of practice I have come to realize that very often what psychotherapists profess is not in fact what they do, and that what they believe is helpful is not necessarily the most important part of what they are doing.

In the beginning of my practice I found it difficult to assume that what I did would actually be helpful to people. I remember seeing my first few patients, away from the institutional protection of hospital and university, within the context of my own practice. I wondered how my opinion, my prescription, my advice, my listening, and my talking could really be of help to them. At first I felt awkward that they or their insurers would pay me for such simple services. However, as the years passed, and as I spent months and even years working closely with patients and trying hard to understand and to help them, I began to see that something that was happening between us was being helpful to them. I saw them change and grow, often losing the symptoms that had brought them to me, even changing in personality and character in ways which neither of us had expected. As I came to trust the validity of these changes, I wanted as much as possible to understand the causes of them.

Toward the end of my training in psychoanalysis, walking to lunch with one of my colleagues, I turned to her and said: "We have been talking about the factors which help in psychoanalysis. You have been in analysis now for seven years. Has it helped you?" She thought only a moment, then replied: "Yes, it has." "What has helped?" I asked. She paused again before responding. "He never let me down; he was always there and I could count on him to do whatever he said he would do."

Of course that answer was only a beginning, but it made me aware of one quality in a therapist which would be of importance to most patients. I asked other people what they had found to be therapeutic in their treatment. I asked people who were or had been in psychotherapy or psychoanalysis with myself or with others. I asked myself the same thing about the psychoanalysis I had while training to be a psychoanalyst. I asked both relatively normal people who had entered treatment because they needed to do so as part of their professional training, or who had had vague dissatisfaction with their lives; and I asked people who had been floridly psychotic, admitted against their will for treatment in a psychiatric facility. The replies which I have received and my own experience have led me to the conclusions which are the subject matter of this book. I have learned to understand what it is that occurs between people in psychotherapy, and in life, which is therapeutic, and that this is the essence of the psychotherapeutic process.

As I developed my understanding of how the best results could be obtained in psychotherapy, I also came to see a whole range of problems which too often arose in the practice of psychotherapy, to its detriment and to the disadvantage of both participants. This was especially clear in the practice of psychoanalysis. Sigmund Freud, attempting to make the new discipline scientific, had cautioned its practitioners to be objective, reflecting back what the patient said, as would a mirror, or operating in a "clean and sterile" field, without excessive personal involvement, as would a surgeon. This sensible and well-meant advice had been perverted, over almost a century of practice by those who followed him, to something he could never have intended. Psychoanalysts and psychotherapists often became ridiculously unresponsive to their patients. When they should have been caring human beings who worked hard to understand and to help people in trouble, they became cerebral pseudoscientists who trained their patients to accept their neglect of them. It is clear from reports by those who were treated by Freud and his early followers that their patients were not treated in this way. Freud was an emotional, driven, complex, garrulous man, and conducted analysis in that fashion. Many of those who followed him, fifty or seventy years later, have reduced what he had done and written about to a sham.

This misinterpretation of Freud's teachings has led to rigidity in psychoanalytic societies. It has created discord among psychoanalysts and, in turn, imposed severe limitations on the practice of psychoanalysis.

One of the problems in psychotherapy which I recognized as most prevalent was the growth and perpetuation of numerous small pieces of behavior on the part of many therapists. These had to do with how and when the therapist would or would not speak, how bills were paid, how vacations were dealt with, and so on. What should have been relatively unimportant matters assumed great significance, so that many therapists became stilted and artificial in their dealings with patients, with one another, and with others.

I realized that in the course of my own psychoanalysis and psychoanalytic training I had become less responsive and more withholding than I had ever been before, and that this had had a deleterious effect upon my work with patients. Fortunately, this new way of being did not feel right or natural to me, so that it was not very long lived, and I soon returned to behaving as I had done before. I felt intuitively how people wanted, needed, and deserved to be treated, and that was how I dealt with them. I understood that a patient in treatment has a greater rather than a lesser need to be treated in a caring, spontaneous, and genuine way. It was not entirely easy to make this transition, since I was hesitant to leave those established principles which were supported by many of those who taught me. There is a natural conservatism to the practice of science, and that is a necessary safeguard. However, I came to feel that an unwarranted orthodoxy prevailed, based upon habit and safety, rather than upon merit, and that I needed to trust more, once again, in what I felt instinctively to be correct.

As I moved away from the artificial constraints which common practice presented as a model, I felt freer to do psychotherapeutic work in a natural way: this led me to feel that *all* of us who practice psychotherapy were in need of liberation. What concerned me was that patients were disparaging the efforts of psychotherapists who had come under the sway of these unduly inhibiting principles. As a result, several things ensued. The practice of traditionally based psychotherapy, including psychoanalysis, had fallen into considerable disfavor, even disrepute. The public, joined by professionals (including medical practitioners), were seeking other sources of help. A host of therapists and pseudotherapists had devised "freer" practices, some of which were appropriately more liberated, but many of which were an excuse for unhelpful license. All of these factors threatened the well-being and future of the serious practice of psychotherapy.

Another problem which I came to recognize is that psychotherapists, rather than being the realists which they ought and need to be, have often become very much out of touch with the world. Part of this has been because of their own sense of helplessness and guilt which has arisen because they do not feel that the work they are doing is worthwhile or useful. Part of it is because, spending too much time being idealized by their patients, losing all sense of proportion and humor about themselves, they develop a false self-image of omnipotence which nonetheless they find comforting. The inappropriateness of such attitudes is illuminated by the words of L. Frank Baum, as follows:

> Promptly at nine o'clock the next morning, the green-whiskered soldier came to them, and four minutes later they all went into the Throne Room of the Great Oz. . . . Presently they heard a Voice, seeming to come from somewhere near the top of the great dome, and it said solemnly:
>
> "I am Oz, the Great and Terrible. Why do you seek me?" . . . Toto jumped away . . . in alarm and tipped over the screen that stood in a corner. As it fell with a crash they looked that way, and the next moment all of them were filled with wonder for they saw . . . a little, old man, with a bald head and wrinkled face, who seemed to be as much surprised as they were.
>
> "I am Oz, the Great and Terrible," said the little man, in a trembling voice, "but don't strike me—please don't!—and I'll do anything you want me to . . . I have been making believe."
>
> "Making believe!" cried Dorothy. "Are you not a great Wizard?"
>
> "Not a bit of it, my dear; I'm just a common man."
>
> "You're more than that," said the Scarecrow, in a grieved tone, "you're a humbug."
>
> "Exactly so!" declared the little man . . . "I am a humbug."

"I think you are a very bad man," said Dorothy.

"Oh, no, my dear; I'm really a very good man; but I'm a very bad Wizard, I must admit."

What does the story tell us? First, that we want to have wizards who can perform magic to help us. Second, as the Wizard himself later explains, otherwise well-meaning common men such as himself can get drawn into meeting this expectation on the part of others and, once having done so, find it difficult to change their role. Third, when the disguise drops away, those who have been deceived are justifiably angry and disillusioned. But fourth, and most important for us, when such humbug is put aside, a common man can be most helpful with common problems, as the dethroned Wizard later proved.

These are some of the problems within the practice of psychotherapy which have developed over the past half-century. This work, when well performed, is of enormous importance to society and especially to some of its members, who, when in difficulty, cannot be helped in any other way. But there is an important need for change in this field. One way to bring about change is through destroying the system; this is reckless, and leads to anarchy. The other is through modifying what exists, markedly, explicitly, but in an evolutionary way. This is what I am proposing. For if psychotherapy does *not* change significantly, it will wither as a discipline. If it *does* change in more positive directions, it will become once again the creative pursuit it was in the early years of its development. I am optimistic about the possibilities for such change. But if it is to come, it will only do so after much painful confrontation of the issues to which I have alluded.

Psychotherapy is not a perfect tool. The value of any tool lies in the use to which it is put. It is, in some ways, the most exciting experience in which people can engage. Psychotherapy cannot provide solutions to all problems, but one can reasonably expect that when it is well employed a great deal can be accomplished in the service of the fuller development of the individual human being.

What follows aims at creating a realistic understanding of the psychotherapeutic experience.

LOVE'S
LABOR

1

THE PENDULUM SWINGS
Psychotherapy Today

IN THE past forty or fifty years, a marked change has taken place in the Western world, particularly in the United States, in attitudes toward the practice of psychotherapy. At the turn of the last century, Sigmund Freud developed that intensive form of individual psychotherapy called psychoanalysis. It was characterized by the fact that the patient lay on the couch, the analyst sat behind him, they met most days of the week, and the patient was encouraged to talk freely about all that he had experienced, felt, thought, and dreamed. The brilliance of Freud's writings in this field caught the imagination of intellectuals in many different disciplines, and psychoanalysis was seen as a new hope for a better society in the future. Freud himself remained reserved, even pessimistic, about the ultimate contribution which could be made to mankind by this new form of human activity. At the end of his life he was gloomy about the extent to which change in people could come about.

Others who followed Freud were not as restrained. What began as a relatively simple arrangement: two people coming together, one trying to help the other by taking that entire person into account, became much more complex. Psychoanalysts needed to define themselves, so they formed societies. They needed to reproduce themselves, that is, train and recognize other analysts, so they founded psychoanalytic institutes. Petty rivalries developed and flourished. The inevitable bureaucracy that develops in human institutions came into being, and the members, as is so often the case, became arrogant and insular. This came to have a deleterious effect upon the practice of psychoanalysis itself.

Freud made a unique, creative contribution to something that has always existed in all societies: there have always been physicians, priests, shamans, and wizards to counsel, guide, and instruct those in trouble or in pain. Psychoanalysis was an important and serious attempt to bring the scientific method to bear upon such endeavors.

Whereas psychoanalysis was developed in Europe, first in Vienna where Freud did most of his work, and then in London where he spent his later years, it was in America that it had its greatest flowering. This is not surprising, for both science and humanism have always been important in American society. In addition, the United States responds more fully to changes than do other more conservative societies. Before, during, and after World War II, a wave of European psychoanalysts came to America. Their ideas took hold and penetrated many corners of American life. When I trained as a psychiatrist in the early 1950s, psychoanalysis had an enormous influence upon American psychiatry. Almost all chairmen of university departments of psychiatry were psychoanalysts. The great majority of residents training in psychiatry also sought concurrent training in psychoanalysis. Institutes were besieged with applicants, and those fortunate enough to be accepted were grateful and proud. But as is often the case, the pendulum swung too far in one direction. Many psychiatrists, through the influence of psychoanalysis, lost their appropriate connection with medicine. The value of other treatments, including hospital care, electroshock, and medications was unduly disparaged. A split of major dimensions occurred between psychiatry and medicine, as many psychiatrists, basically believing that psychological treatment was the only pure and effective treatment, withdrew quietly into their consulting rooms and shut out the real world.

When I was an intern in New York City in 1953, and was considering training in psychiatry, a fellow intern said to me: "Of course you will also want to train in psychoanalysis—otherwise your work would be dull and useless." I was taken aback by this opinion, and by the condescension toward all other forms of treatment which it revealed. Predictably, the overswing of that pendulum was eventually reversed. In the nineteen-fifties, sixties, and seventies important breakthroughs came in other areas. Tranquillizers, antidepressants, and Lithium emerged and were found to be effective. At the same time, society was challenging traditions and conventions, thus creating a climate in which quicker, more emotional, and active forms of psychotherapy emerged. As a result, psychoanalysis fell from favor. The majority of bright young residents wanted training in the more medical aspects of psychiatry, and openings for training in major psychoanalytic institutes became difficult to fill. At the same time other professionals, especially social workers and psychologists, took an increasing interest in psychotherapy. They began to practice privately, and to refer patients to one another; this further diminished the psychotherapeutic portion of the practice of psychiatry, especially in the major American cities.

In spite of this excessive swing of the pendulum in the opposite direction to that which I first described, the fact remains that psychotherapy will always be needed as one of the essential ways in which human beings help one another. An example of such need is the story of Jane, a seriously ill patient, who could not have recovered with any other form of treatment:

Jane, a woman in her early thirties, had been a patient in a psychiatric ward over a period of two years. She had been terribly ill, the most prominent symptom of her illness having been hopeless depression. She had made repeated, serious, violent suicidal attempts. She had swallowed poison and cut her wrists. Finally she had planned to buy a gun and shoot herself. Her life had been saved numerous times by rigorous medical intervention. Between suicide attempts she had repeatedly begged to be allowed to die.

Jane's treatment was tremendously demanding for the staff on the ward, but they did not give up. For months she needed to be constantly in the company of a nurse, around the clock. She was given medication, and for a time, electroshock treatments. She was also seen briefly every day by a psychiatrist. The perseverence of the ward staff—nurses, doctors, social workers, and occupational therapists, finally began to convince her that life might be worth living. Gradually, she allowed herself to speak with them, to share some of her terror and anguish. Over a period of many months she became more settled, more sure of herself, increasingly stable. Eventually she was able to be discharged, and continued to be seen as an outpatient by a psychiatrist for several months.

After having been out of the hospital for almost a year, Jane was working successfully and her life was much more satisfying. She was no longer in constant pain, having learned to respect herself and to be less self-blaming. Because she had come to be more aware of her feelings about people she became more selective in her choice of friends and thus more able to develop lasting relationships. Some time after her discharge, Jane came to visit the staff in the hospital, who were most impressed with her progress. She embraced one of the doctors she had not seen since leaving the hospital. "Thank you," she said, "for not giving up on me. Thank you for not sending me off to a chronic hospital when I was ill for so long. I am very grateful."

Jane might easily have become a chronic patient, a hopeless resident of the back ward of a mental hospital. What saved her from that fate was a human, caring, insightful, and dogged approach on the part of those who were responsible for her care. Their attitude, that there was nothing that dictated that she needed to remain ill, played an important part in her recovery.

The basic and essential part of Jane's treatment was psychotherapy. Earlier I described briefly that most intensive form of psychotherapy called psychoanalysis. Despite the many problems attending the growth and development of psychoanalysis, there have been some very useful developments, too. A group of practitioners, mostly American, modified and adapted psychoanalysis into a less intensive form of treatment known as psychoanalytically oriented psychotherapy or dynamic psychotherapy. It was this that formed the basis of Jane's treatment in the hospital. This treatment can be highly effective, and it is the principal one discussed in this book. At the same time, what I say about this adapted form of psychoanalysis will also apply to psychoanalysis itself, for in both instances the reasons that the patient improves are the same.

Dynamic psychotherapy will usually be conducted face-to-face, rather than making use of a couch. It will involve meeting one or more times a week (psychoanalysis would involve more frequent sessions). As with psychoanalysis, the goal is to explore the patient's life as much as possible. The principal task of the patient is to make herself known to the analyst. She will talk about all manner of things—her thoughts, feelings, actions, life history, dreams, and problems. As therapy progresses and trust is established there should be almost nothing which the patient feels unable to express. The therapist has a reciprocal task. In order to promote a trusting relationship she must behave in a manner that allows the patient to discover that self-exposure is safe. It is necessary for the therapist to accept within herself the total person who is the patient so that her feelings toward her are largely positive. Acceptance at that level will be instinctively recognized by the patient and will free her to become increasingly successful at self-revelation.

One of the basic premises on which the treatment is based is that many of the patient's thoughts and feelings are beyond her awareness, and a major aim of the analysis is to bring this material from being unconscious to a level of awareness where it may be examined and explored. The patient will find, as she becomes increasingly aware of her previously buried beliefs, fears, and emotions, that her conflicts and tensions will be reduced.

As well as facilitating the desired freedom of expression by being a good listener, the therapist must contribute directly to the patient's understanding of the material which is being revealed. These contributions can take many forms, from simple clarifications to more lengthy interpretations in which partly hidden feelings are explained in terms which are consciously understood. Understanding also comes from other sorts of interventions on the part of the therapist, from statements and queries, from agreements and disagreements, from laughs, from silences, and from expressions of surprise or sympathetic understanding; in short, from all her human responses. It is not the therapist who discovers and announces the truth, it is the patient who ultimately can confirm, by her own responses, that which is true for her.

PSYCHOTHERAPY TODAY

Despite the ongoing criticism of psychotherapy, there are at present in the United States and to a lesser extent in other Western countries, more paid psychotherapists, both in actual number and per capita, than at any previous time in human history. Therefore, a greater percentage of the population must be taking the time and paying the money to be treated by a therapist. What has led to this situation? It has been suggested that our society is especially noxious, so actively weakening or sickening its members that increasingly we all require therapy. These noxious elements have included insecurity because of the threat of global nuclear war, economic vulnerability because of inflation and recession, alienation because of a loss of commitment to a close family structure, disaffiliation of each generation from each preceding one, and the narcissism engendered by insufficient structure and limits in the rearing of the young. In all likelihood each of these concerns has some merit but none is totally explanatory. Suffice it to say that our time is unique in some ways, but probably less unique than we tend to believe.

It would be satisfying if we could explain the present proliferation of psychotherapists by saying that the pressures of present-day life created a greater need for therapists, that society then trained them, and that people then made good use of a new and needed resource. I am afraid it has not been that simple. First of all, because of the enormous demand, incompetent as well as competent therapists have been produced. Secondly, psychotherapy has been overidealized with more expected of it than could possibly be delivered. This idealization of psychotherapy resulted in the expectation that therein lay the salvation of society. This view maintained, in essence, that if only enough attention were paid to, and use were made of psychotherapy, all manner of problems would be soluble, or even better, avoidable.

The effects of this attitude have assumed a variety of forms. Psychiatrists appear in courtrooms, three for the plaintiff and three for the defendent, each soberly giving his "expert" opinion; and the entire exercise is immediately open to ridicule and dismissal because the opinions are so contrary that they cancel each other out. Psychohistorians cast a backward glance at the personal history of political figures and reinterpret events in the light of their supposed conflicts and neuroses. Psychologists analyze candidates for political office, whom they have never met, and make pronouncements which are expected to influence the choices exercised by voters. And, even more common, hosts of professionals tell "how to" in articles aimed at the public; how to live, how to rear children, how to work, and how to have sexual relations. A generation of such experience has contributed, at least in some people, to an erosion of confidence in their own ability to do anything without professional assistance or guidance. However, the lack of confidence resulting from this dependency on experts is not in itself an indication of the need for psychotherapy. This leads us to the question: who *does* need psychotherapy?

While it is not possible to draw up a list of specific criteria that will say who is and who is not in need of psychotherapy, it should be possible to draw up some general guidelines. However, we must not move to such a perception of personal incompetence that we believe that all difficult decisions in life must be made in the company of an expert. One becomes adept at meeting the challenge of life by developing one's own capacity to choose and to decide. Few choices are right or wrong in a black-and-white way. Both children and adults should be encouraged to make choices and select options. Professional advisers should not be endowed with greater wisdom and foresight then they do indeed possess. Nor should people be encouraged to believe that life without discomfort is attainable or even desirable. There is no form of psychotherapy, however successful, which leads to a life free of stress and pain. The most that a person can achieve is to learn to cope with life in adaptive rather than maladaptive ways, so that he can make choices which are least likely to cause unnecessary discomfort and can encompass and survive unavoidable discomforts when they do occur.

A person who is psychotic, who is deluded and hallucinating, clearly requires professional help. He may very well need to be in a hospital until he is no longer a danger to others or to himself; he may require medication to reduce tension and other major symptoms; he would also benefit from psychotherapy.

On the other hand, when individuals break down, or threaten to, in the face of overwhelming acute stress, they may or may not require such help. A loss through death, separation, or divorce is the greatest loss that a person can experience. The human organism is programmed, when such a loss is sustained, to suffer a series of emotional reactions which take both time and energy on the individual's part. Professional help is not always needed, or even advisable, but it can be of great help in many instances.

A third group of potential psychotherapy patients, about whom it is most difficult to make decisions regarding treatment, are those who are neither overtly severely disturbed nor suffering acutely from a severe life loss. Such people have the feeling that life is not satisfactory. They are either not successful enough or, even though they may be successful in the eyes of the world, they see themselves as failures. This leaves them feeling frustrated and empty. In some cases they wonder whether psychotherapy would be of help. For this group, short-term therapy lasting a few weeks or even a few months will not suffice. The patient will need extended treatment over a period of several years.

It is amongst this group that one finds some of the most rewarding candidates for psychotherapy, since they are able to use the time and the skills of the therapist to the best advantage. Though their discomforts may not be visible to others, they may suffer from chronic feelings of hopelessness, depression, and despair. Such patients are often people of great inherent value who are unnecessarily uncomfortable and whose abilities are insufficiently used: after therapy their zest for life and sense of fulfillment in living can be markedly enhanced.

Barbara, in midlife, had no taste for life. She blamed herself for all that was wrong with her. She did not enjoy living, and longed for life to end. She made suicide attempts, clear evidence of her sense of defeat. She was always lonely, in spite of being a gifted person who worked with much success with others in an artistic capacity. She wondered for years whether therapy might help her, but felt it probably could not, and doubted that it would be warranted for a therapist to take the time to treat someone like herself.

When she had been in treatment with me, once a week for six years, Barbara recalled our first meeting together: "I remember very clearly my first visit to you. I was in a terrible state of depression and very nervous as to whether or not you would accept me as a patient. You listened carefully to all that I spilled out. Then you said you felt that you could help me and that we would talk together and you would take me through my life. I wondered how you would do that. I felt I remembered little about my life and what I did remember seemed boring and insignificant." Barbara went on to say how relieved and touched she had been that I wanted to help her, and concluded by saying: "That was the beginning. We set out on our journey together and we have come a long way."

That journey might easily never have been undertaken. People such as Barbara are proud and independent in how they portray themselves to others: often their pain is known only to them. It would be very easy to conclude that they are not in need of help. But one hour a week over a number of years offered us the opportunity to explore all of Barbara's feelings, concerns, and pain and led in the end to the development of someone who was able to live with considerable pleasure and to work more effectively than ever before.

When asked how psychotherapy had contributed, not only to her sense of well-being, but to her effectiveness in the field of the arts, Barbara told me the following story:

"I had always been a successful teacher, my pupils were well known, often famous, and my teaching ability was, in my eyes, my only major asset. What gave me the courage to seek help from you was a traumatic experience which threatened my whole professional life. I had been ill for some time and unable to teach. I sat down one day to prepare a class before returning to work. After staring at a blank page for several hours I realized to my horror that nothing would come. That experience is a far cry from my present situation. I am now able to approach my life and my work quite differently. I have learned, first of all and most importantly, to respect myself. In the past I had little or no life apart from my job. It was all-absorbing, physically exhausting, and served as an excuse for not recognizing my pain and loneliness and that most of my relationships were unsatisfactory. Had I been aware of how I felt I would have blamed myself for expecting too much from life and from others. Now I make time for myself, know what I enjoy, choose friends whom I can trust, and do not feel compelled to tolerate behavior which is repugnant to me. I can allow myself some human failings, although

this is still difficult. Dislike of myself was one of my strongest unrecognized feelings, and it has taken me years to believe that I am not such a bad person after all. I know that I am honest, generous, and that I have integrity. I can also allow that I am voracious, sometimes manipulative, and intolerant. In terms of my work I am much more relaxed and more positive. This affects everything I do, including my teaching.

"I still have difficulty confronting staff members when they behave in a way which I feel is harmful to the students or the institution which I head. However, I improve with practice. Also, I find that being able to express more freely how I feel is not only a relief to me but also to the person concerned. Although it hurts, I think we all feel better when we know where we stand. Therapy has taught me exactly where I stand with regard to myself and others. That knowledge has certainly made me a better 'boss.' One important side effect of psychotherapy, although it was never discussed is the fact that I no longer suffer from claustrophobia."

The patient who seeks psychotherapeutic help is indeed in a vulnerable position. In all likelihood he will not know any therapists personally, so he must rely upon other sources for information or referral. Many patients have said to me: "I don't want just to pick a name out of the telephone directory." The fortunate patient will have a family physician or physician–friend who has good judgment about psychotherapists. Those who are less fortunate should try to find the name of a good consultant in psychiatry: one who is known both as an experienced psychotherapist and as a person active in his other professional work.

A consulting therapist must decide on the basis of meeting with the patient, whether therapy might help. I almost always reach my decision after one hour's consultation with a patient, although in a very complicated situation where someone has a long history of disturbance and treatment, several diagnostic consultations may be advisable. I believe that the number of patients who *cannot* be helped is small. So, when a patient actively seeks therapy, in the very large majority of instances I conclude that he would derive some benefit from treatment. The next part of the consultant's task is more challenging: that is, to suggest the appropriate form of treatment and to help find a suitable therapist.

Psychotherapy is a most personal and individual matter. It is not a technique which is learned, then applied identically to all comers—as, for example, in the determination of blood pressure or in the removal of an appendix. On the contrary, the therapy is based on a highly idiosyncratic factor, that is, the relationship between the two personalities involved. A consultant cannot be sure which two people *will* work well together. But his brief experience with the patient, and his longer experience with his colleagues, should enable him to say which combination might very well be expected to work out well.

When no referring physician is available to suggest a therapist, a patient or former patient may be helpful. Having experienced psychotherapy he will be in a good position to advise on his therapist's experience and on his sincerity. One must beware, however, of the excessively zealous patient, who, having been allowed unrealistically to idealize his therapist, may well recommend him with unwarranted enthusiasm.

Thus far, in talking about who needs psychotherapy, I have discussed those who are severely ill, those who require brief treatment because of one of life's losses, and those who can best use some years of treatment for slow, steady, and major results. There is yet another group of patients who will benefit from psychotherapy. They are people who, without treatment, cannot manage life, and end up either withdrawing at home or being repeatedly or chronically hospitalized. These

people can be helped sometimes, with occasional psychotherapeutic intervention, to stay in the mainstream of life or at least
along its edges. Some consider this a waste of time, energy,
and money. It is not. Much pain can be alleviated or pre-
vented in this way by virtue of a very limited investment of
time. The savings, not to the individual alone, but to all society, through such preventive work, are enormous.

So who, then, needs psychotherapy? Not everyone, but
certainly some people. And of those who need it, there is no
formula for how often and how long is best. Good psychotherapy will lead to growth and development and further individuation in the patient, as illustrated by these examples of three
patients whose treatment was successful:

*A seventeen-year-old girl comes for treatment. She is habituated to
several drugs, has been admitted to three hospitals, has failed at
school. She has made several abortive suicide attempts, and is es-
tranged from her family. After being seen once a week for five years
she holds a steady job, is unhappy only rarely, has good friends, and
has a stable relationship with her family. Three years later she is a
leader in her chosen field, happily married, and excited by the pleasures and prospects of her life.*

*A thirty-year-old woman, married to a lawyer, is seen in the emer-
gency room of a general hospital. She is cowering with fear in the
throes of an acute psychotic break, which is the first she has experienced. The psychosis clears with outpatient antipsychotic medication and support.*

*She continues in outpatient psychotherapy, once a week, dealing
with the problems in her marriage and her intense anxieties, fears,
and depressiveness, all of which, she becomes aware, have existed
throughout her life. After another three and a half years she does not
need medication, and only occasionally feels depression that lasts
more than a few hours. Her life is socially active and she is preparing*

for a new career. She says that she feels secure within herself in a way she has never known, and can hardly believe how different she feels herself to be.

A fifty-year-old man is an acknowledged leader in his profession, but he is chronically suicidal. He has always worked successfully, and has always felt let down by others. He has been full of self-doubts and anxieties, though others may have seen him as justifiably self-assured. He is very lonely, feeling that he has no friends. He is certain that his life is running downhill.

He is seen once a week for six years, then gradually cuts back to one visit a month. He finds his life satisfying now, sometimes even exciting. He chooses as friends those few people who he finds can show serious interest in him, values them, and feels they value him. He says: "For the first time now I am glad to be alive."

It is clear from these examples that a good experience in psychotherapy leads the patient to a richer and more satisfying life. In these days of doubt and conflict the psychotherapist and his work are of great import to our society; wherein he succeeds, he makes a significant contribution to that society; wherein he fails, not only does he disappoint that society but, all too often, does it a serious disservice.

2

SIX ATTRIBUTES IN SEARCH OF A THERAPIST

WHEN one questions patients and therapists carefully, one finds that certain attributes when found in a therapist are especially important. Before I describe these attributes, it is worth wondering what gives them an importance that is agreed upon by virtually all patients. The answer is, simply, that these are the qualities that all human beings need, and hence yearn for, in other human beings.

EMPATHIC CONCERN

Each Thursday morning I "make rounds," accompanied by a group of colleagues, on an inpatient psychiatric service in a general hospital. I briefly interview both new patients and those who present problems which are especially challenging.

I was once asked to see an eighteen-year-old girl. Joan had been treated briefly in several hospitals. She had made a number of serious suicide attempts and was taking numerous drugs. She was admitted to our ward because we were willing to work with her on a long-term basis to see whether that would succeed where her briefer admissions had failed.

In her first few days at the hospital Joan had been angry, rebellious, and attacking. She refused to come to the ward lounge to see me, so I went to her room and found a thin, dark-haired girl with angry eyes. She looked at me briefly and disdainfully: "What do you want?" she threw at me and then withdrew into herself. I offered her my hand and said: "I'm Dr. Greben." She looked at me, hesitated, and gave me her hand, which was damp and cool, then instantly withdrew it.

Like a cornered animal she cast furtive glances at me. Although frightened, she was clearly taking in all that was happening.

"May I sit down?" I asked.

"Do what you like," she replied. "You can go to hell as far as I'm concerned."

I sat down and waited, she looked me over.

She reminded me of numerous people whom I had known. Their pain was caused by their desperate need for someone to break through their defenses and yet, at the same time, they were terrified of that happening. Because they had been hurt so much in their dealings with others, they no longer expected to be understood. Instead they were always trying to protect themselves from further hurt by not allowing anyone to come close to them. I suspected that was how Joan felt.

"What do you want?" she said in a tone of challenge.

I hesitated and then smiled and said: "I want to talk to you but you sure make it difficult." There was no response. A few moments later I ventured another question: "How did you get into this position?"

"What position?" she asked.

"You are very good at attacking people and in that way you are able to keep them from knowing who you are."

"You can go to hell," she repeated, eyeing me suspiciously.

"See what I mean?" I responded.

She smiled uncertainly, as if not quite sure what to make of me, but I sensed that she was aware that I liked and respected her, and that she was pleased that her efforts to keep me at a distance had failed.

"You are clever and perceptive," I said, a conclusion I had reached by observing her carefully during our brief meeting. As I stood up to leave, I told her to let me know if she wanted to talk at some other time. I smiled and offered my hand. She held it for a moment or two and then I said, "I'll be seeing you again." "Yes, I'd like that," she replied, and I left the room.

I felt that behind the wall which this apparently uncaring and tough young woman had built around herself was a bright, sensitive person. She sensed the empathic concern which I felt for her. She had developed to a fine art a way of telling people to let her alone, to let her be. Had I done so, and just stood off to one side, leaving her to reach out to me, no real contact would have been made. I was able to reach the real person by letting her see how I felt, that I liked her and would not be driven away by her belligerent attitude. This knowledge surprised and pleased her; it was a relief to be perceived as she really was behind her defensive screen. I felt the playfulness and humor behind the angry facade and I understood that her rejection of me was not a personal matter: experience had taught her that people rarely took the time or trouble to understand what was going on inside her. She was afraid to trust anyone because she might once again be badly hurt. As a psychiatrist I posed a special threat, since I would try to know her, and that was a danger against which she must guard. Fortunately I was not convinced, either by her years of destructive behavior or by her rejecting manner, that she was irreversibly damaged, and I believed she could be helped to change. She was not fully aware of this but she sensed my optimism and my positive feelings toward her.

This meeting was not part of Joan's ongoing treatment, which has had excellent results and has involved hard work on the part of many people, including the patient. She was treated on the inpatient service for almost a year, and one major influence in her recovery was the attitude of the staff, all of whom had a continuing interest in her.

They were persistent in their efforts to get to know her, and she gradually learned, through their caring behavior, that it was safe to allow oneself to be known. When she was finally able to leave the hospital she continued with psychotherapy once a week as an outpatient. This helped her to confront those problems that commonly arise when patients leave the protective environment of a hospital and reenter the everyday world.

As for my first encounter with Joan, it is an example of how, by actively reaching out with warmth and understanding a therapist can make contact with a person who is fighting to avoid becoming a patient.

RESPECTFULNESS

When a therapist intervenes with statements or questions, his purpose is to put into words what he and the patient are beginning to understand. Whether he is clarifying, interpreting, or summarizing, his attitude toward the patient should be full of respect. These interventions may be brief, such as "Yes," in assent to a patient's speculative musing about the meaning of his behavior, or much longer explicit explanations may be appropriate. Both are important in the search for the truth. The silent, rarely interpreting therapist shows disrespect for his patient, who naturally resents him because this relationship mirrors that of a powerful parent and an excessively dependent child.

As I mentioned earlier, Freud first encouraged the analyst to be like a mirror, reflecting back what the patient said. There was a good reason for this advice: it seemed important to caution the therapist against getting in the way of the free flow of the patient's thoughts and feelings. Unfortunately, passive silence became, in time, a dogma amongst many therapists who, leaving all of the work to the patient, neglected the active

part which they themselves needed to play in the psychotherapeutic dialogue.

*Allison was a social worker who had practiced therapy for about
twelve years. I met her when I conducted a seminar on being therapeutic in which I asked any of the participants who had been in
psychotherapy to discuss their experiences as patients. Allison told
us of her only such experience:*
  *Years before she had recognized that she had deep feelings of
anxiety and apprehension in connection with her work. She was a
conservative and reticent person who regretted that she was unmar-
ried and often felt lonely. She went to a psychoanalyst for help. This
is how she described her experience. "When I arrived he greeted me
and motioned me to a chair. Since I am an experienced interviewer I
knew that he needed to know why I had come and something about
my past. As I spoke, he leaned back in his chair, put his feet on the
desk and lit a cigar; except for an occasional "uh-hum," he was
silent. At the end of the hour he told me I needed psychoanalysis
and that he was willing to see me four times a week. I said I would
think about it and let him know. I did not go back."*

As a result of this bad experience, Allison never again
sought treatment, although she could have significantly improved her life and her feelings about herself. An opportunity
had been lost because of the insensitive way in which she had
been treated.

While the therapist said virtually nothing, he did a great
deal which spoke for him: he was unresponsive, his casual
attitude showed arrogance and a lack of respect, and his refus-
al to give any explanation as to why Allison should have psychoanalysis was impolite, particularly since he knew that she
was an experienced therapist. This behavior did not speak to
the person Allison was and to what she needed: however it did
speak eloquently about the kind of person the therapist was

and the way he did his work. It also predicted clearly what a therapeutic experience with him would include. Allison heard clearly what his behavior said, and she made her decision accordingly.

It is not always easy for a therapist to be respectful to his patients. Patients are often difficult and sometimes offensive to others. The attacking patient must not be responded to in kind. Even if his behavior is, by social standards, ugly or frightening, he still needs to be met with respect and liking. Of course, people require limits, and therapists who cannot set limits but are always agreeable and accommodating will be of very little use to their patients.

There are many ways in which a lack of respect can be expressed by a therapist. I know of one hospital where the staff in general took the position that the patient was not to be trusted. Most of their encounters with patients were either punitive or condescending. Unfortunately there are some psychotherapists who, because of a defensive posture of superiority, refer to their patients in a way which shows their disrespect. With such a therapist the sessions will only go well if both parties agree, overtly or covertly, that the therapist is the "healthy" or superior one, leaving the patient to be the opposite.

These attitudes may not appear as obvious aspects of the therapist's personal and professional manner; but too often in the seclusion of the consulting room, disrespect is not far off.

Leslie, a sixteen-year-old boy, was in the hospital for the treatment of severe obsessions and compulsions. He was full of fears: that he had killed or mutilated someone, or had knocked them down as he drove his car, which meant he had to circle back to find out. His many concerns about money included the fear that he had lost some, so he constantly needed to check to see whether this was so. His therapist of a year's duration was leaving him. The patient was being transferred to me, and I was sitting at his bedside having our first exploratory conversation. There was a knock at the door, and the patient's former therapist entered. "I've come to say goodbye," he said to the patient, "and to wish you well." Thereupon he reached into his pocket, drew out a handful of coins, threw them on the floor and walked out of the room.

The patient was shocked and justifiably enraged. I was dumbfounded. I could not believe that someone whose responsibility had been to look after another person could be so cruel. His rationalization was that his action would, ultimately, be in the best interests of the patient. He claimed to have deliberately provoked the patient in order to free him to face certain issues which he had too long avoided. Instead he stunned both the patient and myself with his brutal insensitivity.

I have often thought of this incident over the years. The basic disrespect, the brutality of the therapist's conduct marked it as unusual, but not unheard of. The psychiatric resident in question was not stupid, he had been trained at two excellent universities and psychoanalyzed under the auspices of a renowned institute; yet he remained a largely unhappy and basically hostile person.

The reader may wonder how it is possible for disrespectful therapists to stay in business. There are several reasons for this. Patients usually give therapists the benefit of the doubt. They are vulnerable when they come for treatment and tend to believe that the therapist knows what is best for them. Also, they are demoralized and readily blame themselves when anything goes wrong in their dealings with others. After all, they may argue, it is the therapist's task to help the patient discover what is wrong with his life and how he conducts it.

Many patients interpret a difficult manner on the part of their therapists as an indication of strength. Some therapists encourage this view which suggests that being pushed around by a wise therapist is an experience which leads to growth. In fact it does not help the patient, but serves the therapist's need to be difficult and demanding.

Finally, the therapeutic relationship is of necessity a very private one. The therapist is required to keep confidential that which takes place. The patient is free to say as much as he wishes about what occurs, but most patients do not discuss in depth what happens in their therapy since it is a personal and often painful experience. It may not be until years later that they divulge not only the positive but also the negative aspects of their psychotherapeutic experience.

There are other reasons why a therapist would treat his patient without respect. He may want but fear closeness with that person and adopt an unfriendly manner in order to maintain a safe distance. He may punish his patient because he does not enjoy his work as a therapist. He may even be fearful of the patient's craziness, knowing that somewhere within himself lie the seeds of such madness.

The therapist needs good training, self-knowlege, and self-control if he is to avoid abusing his patients, who are clearly at a disadvantage in the therapeutic situation. A similar relationship exists between parent and child and it is only recently that we have been giving the abuse of children by their parents the attention it deserves. People, including patients and children, flourish when they are taken seriously and their individual rights are recognized. Without this basic respect their growth will be limited.

Patients need to know that it is not always their fault if things do not go well in the treatment. They must also be aware that if what takes place is not satisfactory to them, they have not just the right but the obligation to make a change to another therapist. This is their only alternative if they feel the therapist to be insensitive, neglectful, or even abusive.

Some patients, of course, are repeatedly dissatisfied with any therapist who treats them but this situation is much less common. In such cases the patient may need encouragement to give one therapist a chance to help him fully.

The following encounter between a patient and myself was one in which respectfulness on the part of the therapist was essential if he was to be allowed into the patient's private world:

John was fifteen years of age, a student in high school. He had been admitted to the hospital for psychiatric treatment because he was inaccessible, suspicious, and withdrawn. He was doing poorly in school and both his teachers and his parents felt he might be becoming seriously emotionally ill. He was smiling and agreeable, but he somehow seemed disconnected. It felt as though a great anger, not admitted, rarely manifest, bubbled somewhere below the surface.

John was born in Poland, and his parents had brought him to Canada at the age of five. It was our first meeting:

"How do you like it here?" I enquired.

"Oh, it's very nice," he replied.

"How do you find the people here?"

"They are very nice."

"I understand that you sometimes have trouble with the other kids at school. Why is that?"

"They laugh at me."

"Why do they do that?"

"I don't know."

At this point I could feel how carefully John was trying to keep the conversation safe in order to keep me at a distance. I was having difficulty reaching him.

"What is it like to live in Canada?"

"It is very nice," he replied.

"What is it like to live in Poland?" His eyes widened a bit.

"That is much better."

"Why is it better?"

"The people are nicer, the people are better."

"What are the people like in Canada?" I asked.

"They are not nice. They do not understand."

"Do they make fun of the people of Poland?"

"No."

I began to wonder whether I would be able to reach John and give him the feeling that I wanted, and was able to understand some of the important things that he felt and believed.

"What do you think of the Pope's recent visit to Poland?"

He eyed me very carefully. "It was very nice."

"Are you proud that the Pope is from Poland?"

"Yes."

"What is it like in Poland?"

"It is very nice. People are close together. The country is very beautiful. The people understand me."

"Do you want to live in Poland?" I asked.

"No."

"Does anyone in Canada ever understand you?"

"Sometimes. Maybe you."

"Could I understand you when I've never been to Poland?"

"Maybe. No. Maybe. I think so."

John was different because he had come from another country with another culture. He showed others that he felt this difference by his blanket generalizations which were an attempt to avoid revealing the anger and humiliation he had so often experienced. He did not believe that he could be understood, he expected to be disparaged and humiliated. The only person who would be allowed past his defenses to see the deeper problems which lay within him, would be one who showed a respectful interest in what his world was really like.

REALISTIC HOPEFULNESS

It is a well-accepted fact that failure with one therapist or even several, may be followed by success with another. The reasons for failure can include the theoretical approach of the therapist or his lack of understanding of his patient, but probably the one which is most common is that the therapist gives up.

In recent years numerous authors in the field of psychotherapy have talked of the hopelessness of patients, of how it can lead to symptoms and even eventually to death. Jerome Frank, a psychiatrist, feels that the restoration of morale in the patient is the principal common therapeutic ingredient which all effective forms of treatment share. It is not difficult to keep hope alive when patients are seen for short courses of treatment, but when something more ambitious is being undertaken, as in long-term individual psychotherapy, there is a profound pressure upon the therapist to give up. The patient, convinced that nothing will improve, may assail the therapist with all manner of depressive doubts. Somewhere within himself the therapist will need to have the resources to see that with perseverance, the end of the tunnel will some day be reached. Let me illustrate this point.

Georgina, a woman in her late twenties, was admitted to a psychiatric ward. She was intelligent, attractive, and had a personality which was normally effervescent and highly sociable. She had successfully undertaken several jobs which involved supervising others and had been able to get them to work enthusiastically together.

While in the hospital she had her ups and downs, but as the months passed, it became clear that all of the efforts of the staff were insufficient to keep her from following a slow and steady downhill course.

Nurses, doctors, and social workers liked her. When she was at her better level, whe was much admired by them. She would organize the patients into social groups, arrange parties, and tease the staff in mostly benign and good-humored ways.

When she had been in the hospital for several months a crisis point was reached. Georgina lost hope that she would ever be consistently well again. She made several very serious suicide attempts and, were it not for some good fortune and much hard work on the part of the medical staff, she would certainly have succeeded in taking her life. After one of these attempts she regressed more and more until she was behaving like a terrified and abandoned infant. She stayed in her room, under round-the-clock nursing supervision. She would not speak. She wailed and moaned and tore her hair. She cringed in the corner and whimpered. She begged to be allowed to die.

A meeting of the nurses was called on the ward and I was asked if I would, in order to discuss with them how difficult, even impossible, a problem this was for them. As we talked we could hear Georgina's cries which sounded like those of a young animal, caught in a trap, in terrible pain, yet unable to elicit or even expect help.

"Surely," said one of the nurses, "it must be time for us to admit we have failed. We cannot keep this up day after day. The staff are demoralized, and the other patients are terrified."

"It is a terrible experience for everyone," I admitted. "But what is the worst part of it for all of you?" They thought for a moment. "It is impossible," one replied, "to have to sit with her, witness her suffering, and not know what to do. There is no way that we have of even talking to her, let alone helping her feel better. And it has gone on for so long that we believe now that she can never be well."

"Do you know that?" I asked.

One nurse turned to me. "I have never seen such a patient. Dr. Greben, have you ever seen such a patient?"

My mind went back to similar patients I had known in the past. Some had been depressed and feeling hopeless. Some had had repeated admissions to hospitals. Some had come to my office week after week as outpatients and, as the months and years passed, I had wondered at times whether they could ever be well. I remembered specific people and their individual hopelessness and how, despite the demoralizing times, they had eventually moved ahead and become stronger and ultimately well.

"Yes, I have," I replied.

"Is it possible for such a patient to recover?"

"Yes," I answered. "I have seen a few people who have been this way, and who have recovered completely. Georgina has no process going on within her, such as a genetic, biochemically induced schizophrenia, against which we have to work. She is a person who was born normal, who has suffered many hurts and failures, who has had a good share of accomplishments and successes. She is at her lowest ebb. This is the worst one can feel and still be alive. She has given up. But I have seen people such as this get better." We talked a bit further but I had made the only important point that I could make. No one knew that Georgina would be well. But I knew that she could be well, that behind the wailing infant the vivacious young woman lay intact. She had regressed, to a remarkable degree, but inwardly she had not deteriorated. That is an important distinction.

I went back to my other work, and the nurses and ward staff went on with theirs. Georgina continued to require constant nursing attendance. They tried to talk to her, but when they felt even that was too much for her, they simply sat with her. As more weeks passed she gradually became more settled, and was able to make use of their interest in helping her. The terrible crisis had passed, and the long, slow climb toward recovery proceeded. Several months later, she had gradually and steadily improved so that she could be allowed brief visits away from the hospital. Today she lives on her own, feels happy, works, and sees a therapist once a week, in order to continue the progress she has made.

Georgina came close to being transferred to a chronic care psychiatric hospital. This was not because the people who looked after her were uncaring or incompetent. On the contrary, they were dedicated but defeated. I was in the fortunate position of having gone through similar experiences with other patients. I am sure the nursing staff had many doubts about what I said, but they knew that if I had previously had such an experience which turned out positively, then that could happen again. It was sufficient to allow them to take a deep breath and keep going.

This is a dramatic illustration in that it shows the depths to which the patient sank and the despair felt by those who treated her. Most psychotherapy is not so dramatic, and feelings of despair are quieter and less evident. But probably in the course of all such treatment, points are reached where both parties are discouraged and pessimistic about the value and future of the therapy. At such times it becomes critical whether or not the therapist has reserves of hopefulness on which to draw.

I have not called the quality in question simply "hopefulness" but rather "realistic hopefulness," and this is an important modifier. Those who are cheery and optimistic and always in good spirits regardless of the realities that surround them, have no place trying to do serious work with severely disordered patients. Nothing is more infuriating to a deeply depressed person than to be "cheered up" with the opinion that "everything will be all right." Mindless optimism, rather than being encouraging is discouraging, because the patient feels that the therapist knows neither what he is doing nor with whom he is dealing.

All human endeavor requires strength of spirit, determination, and perseverence, and psychotherapy is no exception. I have often had patients say to me: "This is very hard to do." I have usually replied: "This is probably the hardest thing you will ever do." For the pain of facing discomfiting truths is a special kind of pain. And the finding of the will to continue through months and years of dispiriting confusion is very difficult for the patient. He needs an encouraging therapist but also one who has a good appreciation of reality. It does not help the permanent paraplegic to assure him that he will be able to walk but it *does* help the person suffering from temporary paralysis to hear that with strenuous exertion his condition is probably reversible.

In addition to a realistic goal, a physically disabled person needs from his therapist the personal support and optimism which keep him going when progress is stalled and further attainment seems impossible. The patient in psychotherapy requires the same qualities in his therapist, if he is to accomplish the greatest possible change.

SELF-AWARENESS

The important difference between insight-seeking therapies and other forms of psychotherapy is that in the former not only is it necessary to seek self-knowledge for the patient, but an understanding of the therapist, at least by himself, is essential.

Why is this so? Because what is being sought for the patient is that he will be able to see and to live with the world as it really is—not as he would prefer it to be and not as some other person or people would prefer to portray it.

The psychotherapist comes to the therapeutic situation with his own personal limitations and difficulties. These are his world, and all of us, wherever we go and whatever we do, take our worlds with us. As I have said earlier, many of the therapist's personal characteristics will become known to the patient, but a great deal will remain hidden. Of this hidden part, the more that is known to the therapist, that is the more that he understands himself, the greater chance the therapy has of being successful.

Carla had been in treatment with me for three years. We both agreed that our work together had been both productive and enjoyable. I was planning to be away for a sabbatical year, and we had to decide what she would do at that time. We considered all possibilities, including the fact that she might change to another therapist. In the end we decided that she had come along far enough so that she could see me when I was in town a few times during that year, then resume regular appointments when I returned. Some weeks later we were discussing the matter again.

"Do you feel satisfied with the decision to work together again when I am back?" I asked.

"I do indeed," Carla replied. "I am sure that it is the best solution to the problem of your being away. Why do you bring it up again?"

"Because when we first discussed it you were not entirely sure what to do. In fact at one point you said that you might prefer to change to another therapist."

She paused a moment, then smiled, "That's not really true. You wondered whether I might prefer that. From the beginning I knew I would continue with you." I thought about that. "You are right. I feel it is most important that you do what is best for you. But at the same time I know we have worked well together, and I am reluctant to have you change to another therapist. Therefore I have made it more of an issue for you than it really is."

"I am glad to have that clarified. I knew that it didn't come from me," she said, with some relief.

The patient in therapy is not reacting to just anybody, but to a specific person. When that person, the therapist, knows his own character and vulnerabilities he will be in a position to understand his patient's reactions, and if he is criticized or accused of being unfair, he will be able to judge whether his patient's perception of him is correct or if it is distorted. The work of psychotherapy would be simpler if therapists were always right, and did everything in the best possible way. This is of course not the case. When a therapist makes a mistake, little will be lost if this can be understood and acknowledged. A cynic has said about psychotherapy that "it is the only business in which the customer is always wrong." When this is the case, the results of the therapy will be severely limited.

One patient, whom I have seen once a week for several years, remembers a critical experience in the first months of therapy. She is someone who, despite considerable professional accomplishment, always blames herself for any problems she has with other people. I had explained an aspect of her relationship with her mother, an explanation which she found very painful; as she struggled to make it fit she became concerned because she felt that I was wrong. She phoned me, and, with great difficulty, told me this. I thought for a moment, then told her that she was right and "I was mistaken." She heard this with relief, and we went on from there. It was a simple event. Only several years later did she explain to me that this had been an important moment in the development of her trust in me.

Every therapist has a certain basic style in his manner with people, and he needs to be aware of this, in order to appreciate the effect that he will have upon his patients. My patients, when they know me well enough to speak freely about what they think of my personal style, usually tell me that they find me quiet and basically shy. They suggest that in order to work closely with others I have had to overcome these tendencies. This observation is correct, and when a patient is able to make it, or to comment on other aspects of my personality, I consider their remarks very seriously and agree when they are correct. This does not mean that I accept as correct everything they say. It only means that one of the very real possibilities in therapy is that they might make observations which are not in the least complimentary, and yet may be true. The more I am in a position to know and understand the person whom they are observing and with whom they are dealing, in this case myself, the more I will be able to help them develop a trust in their own capacity to judge and observe both others and themselves.

In his book about psychoanalysis, Ralph Greenson gives an impressive example of candor with a patient. The patient told him that he often talked too much, and tended to exaggerate, and that it got in the way of the patient's freedom to do his work in the analysis. Greenson understood that the patient had indeed made a correct observation about him, and assented to its validity. The analyst's honesty and lack of defensiveness allowed the patient to admire the therapist in quite a different way from the adulation which comes out of idealization. There is another reason for self-awareness in the therapist. He expects his patient to face the difficult task of knowing himself and can only do so with conviction and understanding if he has undergone the same experience.

My view that the therapist should allow himself to become known to the patient, at least in part, differs from what I learned in my training. We were taught that throughout treatment almost nothing about the therapist should be revealed to the patient. In the early part of psychotherapy I agree that this is true. At that time it is essential that a patient is not burdened with too much information about his therapist. In the midst of his pain and confusion, which usually includes the feeling that no one can be trusted, he may not be able to tolerate the knowledge that his therapist is less than perfect. However, as he grows stronger and more sure of himself, he will readily accept that fact and appreciate a therapist who does not try to keep himself hidden.

Marie was in psychotherapy with me for seven years, once a week. When she began she was severely inhibited, fearful, obsessional, entirely wrapped up in her own frightening feelings. In remembering, years later, some of what she had felt early on, she wrote: "There was never any 'We're equal,' 'We both have problems,' etc. I wasn't the therapist's crutch. I knew you must have problems but you didn't bring them to the session, and I honored you for that. It must have been a stress."

As the years in treatment passed, Marie developed more confidence in herself, and was less assailed by doubts as to her worth. As a result, she had less need to idealize me, and was more willing and able to see me more fully.

"There is something I wanted to raise with you," she said after a couple years of therapy.

"What's that?"

"It seems wrong that you call me by my second name, you know me better than anyone ever has."

"How would you feel if I called you Marie?"

"I would feel good if it felt right to you."

"It certainly does—and how about what you call me?"

She thought a moment, and flushed slightly. "I could not call you by your first name. To me you are still Dr. Greben."

"Are you sure that is what you prefer?"

"I am sure. Maybe someday that will change."

At that point Marie wanted us to be closer, but not too close. She was still afraid of too much intimacy, and kept some distance between us. Two years later she had moved even further ahead. I had just made a statement:

"I don't know why you said that," she said.

"I thought it was true, but I was mistaken."

"That's right. You were wrong." She paused as she allowed herself to let it sink in. "I used to idealize you and think you were

always right. I needed someone to look up to, and if I found a flaw in you I would have felt very threatened. To recognize that you were human would have been to risk your failing me and then I would have had to sweep you away with my parents and my brother."

"It is understandable that you were afraid that I would disappoint you: your parents were callous and insensitive toward you. They much preferred your brother, who had no interest in you, and took advantage of the situation. So naturally you were afraid that I too would be unfair to you."

"I'm glad you understand. There was another reason why I had to put you on a pedestal."

"What was that?"

"I was still too frightened to have you anywhere near me."

"You mean you were afraid of where the intimacy would lead us?"

"Yes. So I kept a safe distance by not allowing that you were human."

"Right." I smiled. "Now that I am human, where does that leave you?"

She laughed. "It leaves me in a very good position. We are human together, and that is a pleasure."

"What if you had kept me other than human?"

"I would never have grown up. As I grow up with you, I grow up with everyone. Once I would have found it terribly arrogant to think of myself in the same way as I think of you. Now I feel close to you, and your limits or your problems are part of that. I have learned that there is enough good in you, so that I am able to accept your faults."

"That sounds important."

"It has been. That you are real has been an important part of my growing up. That you realize what you are really like has also been essential."

"Why is that?"

"I cannot tolerate hypocrisy. I cannot accept a double standard. When I first came to you I would have been afraid to hope that you would expect of yourself what you expect of me. Now I know it has to be that way. Otherwise I could not have respected you."

RELIABILITY

It is rare for one person to say about another "he always keeps his word," or as my colleague said about her analyst "he never let me down; he was always there." A therapist who is consistently trustworthy in his dealings with his patients will create a solid basis for the painful and sometimes frightening work of psychotherapy. One of the most important characteristics of people who seek help is their inability to trust others—they are disillusioned because, since infancy, they have been repeatedly hurt and disappointed. The infant is let down when his needs, both physical and emotional, are not satisfied. The child and the adult are hurt, then scarred, by repeated failure on the part of others to take their needs and wishes sufficiently into account. The ability to trust dies finally as promises are broken and justified expectations are not met.

The arrangements which are made in psychotherapy offer a natural test for the reliability of both participants. Sessions take place at prearranged times and their length and the method of payment is clearly defined. Both patient and therapist are then expected to honor those commitments.

Reliability is essential to the development of trust. When psychotherapy succeeds, the therapist will have been reliable in such a way as to have reawakened trust and therefore hope in the heart of the patient.

"Do you know how important it has been that you have been so entirely reliable?"

"Tell me."

"In the first place, I have never been able to count on anyone in all my life. That is a terrible thing to admit, but it is true."

"What have I done that is different?"

"You have kept your word. You have never promised something that you have not delivered. When you are not sure whether you will be able to do something, you tell me that. If I expect something that is impossible, you inform me of that. I can take you at your word, and that gives me a great sense of relief."

"How did you happen to have had such bad experiences throughout your life?"

"I don't know. We have talked a lot about all the important people I have lived with and have known. They always ended up letting me down—not only in major, but in minor ways. You know how many people say: 'We'll have to get together sometime,' or 'I will call you tomorrow,' but they don't do it."

"Elmer Dowd, with the imaginery six-foot rabbit named Harvey, had a good technique. When someone said: 'We must get together soon,' he would immediately ask: 'When?' "

She laughed. "I guess I wasn't smart enough to think of that: and besides, I wasn't self-assured enough. Before I came to therapy I always had the same answer for being constantly let down by other people—it was somehow my fault. In therapy I have learned how unfair that has been to me."

"That is true. You became particularly good at blaming yourself. Now you are more able to see the part that others have played. Tell me, what is the effect within your own feelings of having someone keep his word?"

"It feels fantastic. You cannot imagine what it is like to be constantly hurt or let down by everyone. I guess most people cope with it better than I do—perhaps their experience in childhood was more positive than mine. All I know is that I had lost faith in the possibility that anyone could be counted on for anything."

"Where and how did you decide that I could be trusted?"

"In the beginning I liked your style. You were quiet and serious but very open with me and you had a nice sense of humor. I felt that you liked and respected me and I found that I could rely on you to respond to anything I said without being disapproving or judgmen-

tal. Mind you, at first I was afraid it was just something you had been taught, part of your training—that it said in the textbook that you were supposed to be reliable. So I watched you like a hawk. Finally I was convinced that you wanted to be that way because it felt right and good to you to be that way. That is when I relaxed and really trusted you. Now can I ask you something?"

"Of course."

"Why do you take being reliable so seriously?"

"In psychotherapy so many people have told me how their trust has been violated by others. I have concluded that the solution is not to be found through compulsive, rigid predictability. It is that people need to feel that others care about not disappointing them. To convey such a feeling is extremely important."

STRENGTH

My whole professional life has taught me that a therapist needs to be strong, flexible, and able to adapt to different situations. He should be able to accept discomfort in the hope that it will lead to future comfort, and to forgo instant gratification in order to invest in a distant but more permanent pleasure. A strong therapist operates within a theoretical framework but is not bound by dogma or formulas. To deny the complexity of life and reduce it to such simple terms is an indication of weakness, not strength.

The art of diagnosis may be misused by the therapist who feels comfortable with rules and formulas. Diagnosis is an important tool in medicine, and psychiatry, being a medical specialty, naturally makes use of it, but those who think that by calling someone "hysterical," "obsessional," or even "schizophrenic" they have captured the essence of that person are very much mistaken.

A psychotherapist is armed with the knowledge which he has gained from his training and experience. As he practices his profession he may be dismayed by the number of differences which exist in each patient. If he feels threatened by this discovery there is a danger that he may too readily reach conclusions which are not valid. A strong therapist will, however, be sensitive to the needs of every patient and will treat them as separate and unique individuals.

Strength and courage are required in the therapist to enable him to tolerate exposure to the patient's deepest, strongest feelings, however repugnant he may find them. To adhere to a way of behaving despite evidence that it would be more helpful to reverse that behavior is stubbornness. To be able to change without fear of loss of face is strength. The patient must also be courageous, for he has to face frightening unknowns within himself. A woman, for example, may discover that she cannot stand the child she is supposed to love or that her mother, whom she assumed had cared for her deeply, had actually exploited her for her own selfish ends. Such insights are terrifying and a therapist who is not afraid makes the best companion for the patient who is undertaking that sometimes daunting journey.

A strong therapist does not talk constantly nor is he always silent. Both to speak and to listen require strength. When he is listening, some of what he hears will be disturbing. When he is speaking, his patient may make it difficult for him by resisting the truth which he is presenting.

The therapist needs to be strong enough to let the patient trust him and connect to him and depend on him. At the same time, as the months and years pass in therapy, he must be able to accept his attachment to the patient, and even in some way, his need for and dependency upon the patient.

He must also allow the patient to grow and develop, for that is the purpose of the therapy. As the patient grows, he will in some ways surpass the therapist, who needs the strength to accept this without hesitation. When the time comes he must be able to help the patient separate from him, not completely but substantially, so that eventually the therapy will end. Then he must facilitate the separation, recognizing that the coming of age of the patient represents the greatest gain for both of them, even though each will suffer a sense of loss.

Teresa is a very strong woman. She is a psychologist who is perceived by her friends, her colleagues, and her patients as someone to whom they can look for support and guidance. I met her at a professional meeting, and she told me about the psychoanalysis she had undertaken as part of her training to be a psychoanalyst.

"*Overall it was a fairly good experience, because he was always able to listen carefully and, occasionally, to make helpful suggestions. I realized after a time that he was somewhat intimidated by me: he used to blush when I made things difficult. But that was because he was so uncertain about himself.*"

"*How did you feel about that?*"

"*It was a shock at first, but I accepted it, because he had a good heart. In later years, when I saw him at meetings, he was more experienced, and more sure of himself.*"

"*What about the blushing?*" *I asked with a smile.*

She laughed. "*That was okay. It wasn't his fault. He never pretended to be more than he was.*" *I realized that Teresa had been very disappointed by the vulnerability of her analyst, but had accepted it because other aspects of their work together were good. The blushing was a symptom which betrayed the analyst's discomfort with certain things he heard or felt. Because it was such a visible symptom, that discomfort was readily apparent to his patient.*

"*How did the analysis end?*"

"*Rather well. One day he told me that he thought we could end the analysis pretty soon. He went on to say: 'We have done a lot of good work together. You have gone as far as you can go with me.'*"

Teresa's experience says a lot about the need for different kinds of strength within therapy. In the first place, in many ways she was a stronger person than her analyst. Both of them knew this. It was strength on her part which allowed her, despite this recognition, to work with him and to get as much as she could from that experience. It was strength on the analyst's part that he did not, in the end, deny the true situation, but rather accepted the responsibility for the limits of what they had achieved. This was a generous and genuine way of handling what must have felt very awkward to him.

Any meaningful therapy will be marked, at times, by crises. The therapist will then have to cope with disturbed feelings within himself and the patient. At those times he may incur the wrath or hatred of the patient, the patient's family, or even a colleague. He will not enjoy this and his faith in his ability to make appropriate judgments will be sorely tried. If he is flexible and feels he is wrong, he will back down from the position which encouraged that wrath; but he will not sacrifice his integrity if he feels that he is right and that the storm cannot be circumvented or avoided.

Marjorie was treated in weekly psychotherapy. In the early years she broke down several times into psychotic illness and had to be admitted to hospital on three occasions. At other times, although severely disturbed, she was somehow able to continue her therapy as an outpatient. We worked together on confronting those terrifying feelings which had caused her psychotic breaks—the rage toward her sadistic mother, the anger toward her destructive, attacking husband, the shame over the many hurts and humiliations which she had absorbed during her childhood. Gradually her symptoms lessened and she became less self-blaming and guilty, more able to identify what others had, unjustifiably, done to her. After several years of psychotherapy she said:

"If I had not liked you, which I did from the beginning, I could not have stuck with you at those difficult times when I threatened to quit. And if you had not liked me, which took a bit longer for me to accept, you would not have stuck with me on those occasions when I knew you seriously considered agreeing to send me to another therapist."

On the other hand, she has told me that she has never forgiven me for the fact that I had once had her taken directly from the obstetrical unit of a general hospital (where she had recently given birth) to a psychiatric hospital, without telling her that I was going to do so. She was then on a high floor of the general hospital, and hallucinating and, I felt, dangerously suicidal. She is a woman of very good judgment, and that was the one occasion when I did not share with her the making of an important decision which markedly affected her.

Years later she continued to feel that I had been wrong. I have told her that I cannot be certain, but that I felt it was necessary to follow what seemed like the only safe course at the time of a very dangerous crisis, even though it meant sacrificing for some time, indeed for many years, a portion of her trust and goodwill.

So a therapist must be strong. He must have the strength to say "yes" and the strength to say "no." Like children with their parents, patients in psychotherapy do not improve in a vacuum: they require a relationship with a strong and known person, with whom to share themselves and against whom to measure themselves. The therapist must provide the love and care the patient needs and at the same time set realistic limits for him. This combination should help the patient to develop reasonable self-assurance and the ability to live with what he *cannot* have and to accept what others require. In the minds of some, empathic concern and strength, as demonstrated by limit setting are separated, the former being seen as the quality which resides in the mother, the latter in the father. I disagree. The effective parent of either sex, like the effective therapist, will exhibit in attitudes and behavior both of these highly significant qualities.

In conclusion, I believe that these are the six most important attributes needed by a therapist. In therapy we cannot do without them, for the therapist who lacks these qualities will not win our trust. They give us the sense of being cared for, tended to, valued, wanted, even loved. And these are what, for a lifetime, human beings strive to find.

3

A CERTAIN CHEMISTRY

The Personal Qualities of the Therapist

Some people hold the view that a therapist, being a trained practitioner who has learned to exercise professional judgment, should perform his task without excessive personal involvement. This argument appears to be logical and is in keeping with Freud's injunction to the psychoanalyst to be objective and uninvolved. As mentioned earlier, there were good reasons for his injunction. However, the attitude has been overemphasized by later generations of psychoanalysts. Such a position is not necessarily best across the board, for psychotherapy in all its forms is a highly personal activity and cannot be effective otherwise. It is not just what the therapist does which is important, but who he is and how much of himself he brings to the therapeutic situation.

Most patients who have undergone psychotherapy confirm this view. In the course of therapy they have come to learn a great deal about their therapist and have become aware that who he *really* was and what he *really* valued had been an important influence on them and on the outcome of their treatment. A few patients would feel differently. They were not able to know their therapist because he was virtually silent through several years of therapy. In my experience, patients treated in this way ended up quite uncertain as to whether they had gained much from treatment. If we were to take those patients who felt they had been helped substantially by psychotherapy, we would find that they had perceived it as a highly personal experience which had taken place between two very specific people. In addition, they had come to value very highly that other person. The realization of all of this dawned upon me gradually over the years of practice. After I had been a psychoanalyst for about five years I saw increasingly the damage caused by the dogma supporting unresponsiveness, and I began to give freer rein to my intuitive responses.

Sigmund Freud prided himself on being objective, noninvolved, and neutral; his patients found him subjective, friendly, concerned, responsive, garrulous, and very human. What a strange situation this is! Such a therapist sees himself as more of a technician than a friend. If the patient is persuaded that this is really the case, he will find him sadly lacking and the therapy disappointing, but if, instead, he discovers that the therapist is, like Freud, a warm, caring human being then he will have a good experience in treatment despite the mistaken view of himself held by the therapist.

"I want you to know at the outset, Sigmund, that I am very pleased to have this opportunity to speak with you."

"Believe me when I say that it is my pleasure."

"I hope you will not find me presumptuous in wanting to put some questions to you."

"Not a bit. I will be happy if I can help clear up any problems or misconceptions."

"Good. You see, people today have difficulty understanding the apparent discrepancy between what you wrote and what you did."

"My goodness! They must think that I am a terrible hypocrite!"

"They want to give you the benefit of the doubt. After all, throughout your career you were known for your ruthless honesty and your search for scientific truth."

"Quite so. What is the discrepancy?"

"You cautioned us to be like a surgeon or a mirror, but colleagues and patients did not describe you as functioning in that way. From what I have read it seems that you were very personal in your dealings with them. They found that you betrayed a great deal about yourself in the way you furnished your study: with artifacts, photographs, and mementos. They have also said that you often spoke about yourself and your family at length; that you reminisced about your earlier life, and shared with them your recent pleasures and pains."

"All of that is true. Mind you, I tried not to burden them. I did not see it as their responsibility to be concerned with my troubles, or with finding solutions to them."

"But why did you reveal so much of yourself to them?"

"Why? One has to be human. What else could I do?"

"I see. Did you plan very carefully all that you said?"

"Not really. I pursued my ideas as they came."

"People have indicated that you loved to talk."

(Loud laugh.) "It is true. I love to talk. I always have. Frankly, I find it difficult to stay quiet."

"Did you struggle to say less?"

"Of course not. I struggled to understand my patients, and to evolve theories from what I discovered in them. When I had made such discoveries, I was more than happy to share them with my patients and colleagues."

"But what about the surgeon and the mirror?"

"I always tried to find analogies which would make things clear to my patients, students, and readers. It is easy for people to understand the response to a mirror or the objectivity of a surgeon. It is not so easy for them to grasp what psychoanalysis is all about. I was always afraid of wild analysis—that poor analysts would rush in with instant interpretations before the evidence was in. I wanted to *caution them to observe, to listen, to think about their patients. There have to be standards and principles in all sciences."*

"I see. Look down there. Can you make out that consulting room?"

"Very clearly. Let me see. How strange! The walls are almost bare. There is no life there! How sterile it is."

"The analyst has taken great care not to inject too much of himself into the situation."

"Good Lord!"

"Can you hear what they are saying?"

"I can only hear the patient. He has been speaking since we started this conversation, the analyst has said nothing. Now the hour is over and he only nodded instead of saying a friendly good day."

"Yes."

"What does it mean?"

"It means he is being orthodox."

"Orthodox? Have I created a new religion? Good heavens, is this 'the future of the illusion'?"

"It seems to be."

"I'm leaving. I can't face any more. I warned against certain dangers as I wanted to avoid producing poor analysts. You seem to be telling me that I have created another set of problems which produce something worse—a monster!"

"I hope I haven't offended you."

"Offended? No. Worried? Yes."

"What do you suggest?"

"I suggest nothing. I had my turn. Now it is up to others to straighten out their affairs. I am going back to where I belong. I wish you well."

"Thank you. Goodbye."

One highly gifted psychotherapist was Frieda Fromm-Reichmann. She combined the rare qualities of therapeutic effectiveness with the ability to analyze and describe in her writings something of how she practiced her craft. The somewhat fictionalized account of her treatment by Fromm-Reichmann, written by Hannah Green, was titled *I Never Promised You a Rose Garden*. Some years later Green gave an address: "In Praise of My Doctor—Frieda Fromm-Reichmann" to a group of psychoanalysts. In it she stated: "We had one difference of opinion on which neither of us ever gave ground . . . She held that psychiatry was a science and I said it was an art. She believed that the gifts she had—humor, empathy, indignation, intuition, a first-rate intellect, linguistic sensitivity, and the endearing quality of not exploiting her patients to prove herself or her theories—she believed that these things could be taught and learned, and that anyone who was reasonably intelligent could cultivate them to a degree equal to or exceeding her own. I think she was wrong."

I find the forgoing statement moving and impressive. My own experience in this field has led repeatedly and unavoidably to the conclusion that good psychotherapy is performed by genuine, warm, caring people. As we have seen, the principal goal in therapy is to uncover the real person behind the patient's facade. What we label "psychoneurotic defenses" are nothing more than his efforts to hide his true self in order to protect himself from hurt. The defense which we call "repression" is simply forgetting, both conscious and unconscious, to avoid the pain which remembering will produce. We use the word *dissociation* to describe a defensive measure which allows the patient to remove from his awareness that portion of his psyche which is intolerable to him, thus leaving a changed or diminished part-person.

As so many of such psychoneurotic symptoms are aimed at avoiding pain, then the principal task of the therapist is to find a way around this avoidance. Since the patient is always ready to pronounce dire judgment upon himself from within, it is left to the therapist to create a climate of warmth and acceptance, in which recognition and disclosure of painful facts and feelings can take place.

Although it seems obvious that human beings require warmth from others to feel comfortable, there are, as I mentioned earlier, psychotherapists who do not agree with this view. They believe it is correct to treat their patients in the cool and detached way which has been described, particularly when they are practicing psychoanalysis and their patients are undergoing a personal analysis as part of their training to become analysts. These patients, because of their knowledge of the literature on psychoanalysis, including the writings of Freud, have a fear of being too fully gratified and not sufficiently deprived. Ironically, when they experience deprivation at the hands of an uncaring therapist, they try to comfort themselves and justify his coldness by claiming that he is superior. The child boasting that "My father is tougher than your father" is taking a similar position. In both cases the patient and the child are denying an important part of themselves, the part that longs for and seeks a caring protective figure on whom they can rely.

The grave danger exists that unresponsive therapists, who are also senior analysts responsible for the analyses of analytic candidates in training, will pass on their attitudes. This will then lead to a new "generation" of rigid, uncompromising practitioners whose patients and students will in turn give clear evidence, not of growth and development, but of restriction and narrowness. Because the candidate in a training analysis is being both treated as a patient and trained to become a psychoanalyst, a problem arises if he finds that his analyst is not suitable for him. He is often reluctant to make a change.

Julius was in his final year of psychoanalytic training. He was at an impasse in his personal psychoanalysis and knew that, as a patient, it would be to his advantage to change to another analyst. He said to a friend:

"I am truly stuck in my analysis and neither of us knows what to do. I know nothing more will happen which helps me and I'm fed up with it. The best I can do is to put in my time until I graduate as an analyst and then I'll quickly get out of there."

The analyst of course, was at fault; he should have recognized the impasse and recommended to Julius that he see another analyst.

The majority of therapists are, in practice, active and personal and giving but are not always willing to admit this. As a result, there is a wide divergence between what they do with patients, in their consulting rooms, and what they say at professional meetings or write in professional journals. This is a strange discrepancy. It is not that these therapists are doing *worse* work in private than they will admit in public. On the contrary, they are probably doing *better* work in private, but hesitate to admit this to their peers, for fear that they will be accused of being incompetent, or "wild" or not "classical." Some of them are more aware than others that their theory and practice differ. It is a cause for concern that a therapist might be so unaware of how he functions, but even more serious is if he knows and is too dishonest to admit it.

There are strong pressures within psychoanalytic societies and institutes to conform in thinking to a "classical" view. The analyst who breaks from tradition runs the risk of being seen as heretical. The penalty for this can be either lack of referrals from his colleagues, or, of great importance, not being chosen to be a training analyst. In a seminar to discuss these problems a senior analyst stated flatly that one learns early as a student, and continues to feel the pressure as an analyst to follow the dictum, "Don't make waves." This is hardly an attitude which will encourage scientific discovery and development.

THE PERSONAL QUALITIES OF THE PATIENT

A reliable person coming for treatment evokes quite different feelings in a therapist from an unreliable, unpredictable patient. A patient who is honest and open leads to quite a different quality of therapy from one who is dishonest and evasive. For example, many patients are very accurate reporters of their worlds, and in time the therapist comes to know this. He can then relax somewhat, and trust that what he hears is relatively free of distortion. Some patients tend to distort most things to put themselves in an good light; others do the opposite and present themselves in an unduly poor light. When such distortions occur, the therapist will have to work hard to find where reality lies.

Strength in the patient is another important factor which will contribute toward the success of therapy. There is a widely held belief that people who seek therapy are weak, and that they should be able to work things out for themselves without professional help. This view does not take into account that most people will require the help of another person to be able to recapture those painful thoughts and feelings that have been relegated to the unconscious portion of their minds. Strength and courage are required of the person in order for him to become a patient, to expose himself to another person, to face those uncomfortable truths which will emerge and, finally, to make necessary changes in his life. Even very disturbed patients, contrary to general expectations, often have the necessary strength to succeed in therapy. A patient must be willing to work. It will be seen throughout this book how much effort is involved for both therapist and patient in the process of psychotherapy. If the patient is undaunted by this challenge, then he will move forward, in spite of the setbacks which will of necessity occur. He must also be able to see the part he plays in what happens to him. The patient who is fixed in an attitude of blame toward others will not be able to achieve much change, nor will the patient who only blames himself. In both instances the therapist will try to help the patient move toward a more reasonable attitude so that he can fully understand his contribution to his problems and accept responsibility for his mistakes and faults. Another important quality is generosity; the patient who is basically generous will achieve more in the therapy than the ungiving, selfish patient. Such a quality as generosity is, of course, one facet of character, and I would like now to consider the place of the patient's character in the treatment situation.

Often psychoanalysts have approached their work as though all aspects of the patient's character might be open to change through the treatment. In fact this is not the case. Many therapists have privately agreed that "if you analyze a rogue you end up with an analyzed rogue." Much of what we call character will not be changed by psychotherapy, although the symptom which is the result of conflict may be changed. Two patients, whom I will later describe as Rachael (chapter 8) and Richard (chapter 10) illustrate this point. Because they present themselves to the therapist in such a plausible way, he believes that he will be able to help them. This is not so, for they are basically arrogant and do not want to find out how they are wrong or to work on change within themselves. All they want is to confirm their own belief that everyone else is wrong, needs to change, and should appreciate their superiority.

A basically generous person will seem so both before and after treatment. It is true that before therapy, his generosity may be hidden from the view of all but the most astute observer, but this is because he has been hurt so much that he has inwardly resolved to hold himself back. When he has found ways of being hurt less often by uncaring people, when he has developed a greater capacity to choose friends who are good for him and reject those who are not, he will also show his basic generosity more openly. Warmheartedness, kindness, interest in the welfare of others, honesty, trustworthiness, all of these are established in the early years of life, probably based upon genetically acquired qualities, and will be evident throughout life. Stella Chess and her associates at New York University Medical Center followed a group of people from early childhood over a period of twenty years. Their work strongly supports the view that the genetic basis of temperament.determines characteristics which remain constant throughout life. (I will deal more fully with these matters in chapter 10, on failures, and chapter 11, on good results.) The belief that through therapy people can be changed in every way is an ingenuous one. Therapists must not underestimate their patients' potential for change, but they must be just as careful not to overestimate it.

Fit: The Match between Patient and Therapist

There is a certain chemistry in human relationships which is still unlikely to be reduced entirely to its component factors, despite our great power in science to compute and analyze. It is safe to assume that a therapist can help many quite different patients and a patient can be helped by more than one therapist, but in every instance, once a therapeutic pair has been established, that combination, as in all other intense and intimate human alliances, has its own specific characteristics.

I am often asked to see a patient in consultation with whom I will not be able to continue in psychotherapy. In an earlier chapter I discussed the consultant's task of recommending a therapist to a patient should he feel that the person would benefit from treatment. In part the choice will depend upon who is available. In a small city with only a few psychotherapists, it will not be easy to find one who has time available to accept a new patient. In larger centers there may be a broad choice of people to consider. For the moment, let us put aside the question of availability and discuss the fact that not all therapists will be suitable for a given patient.

Some people behave as though there is no matching required: that any competent therapist could treat any, or almost any patient. This is not the case. Some therapists do better with some patients, and vice versa. The reason for this, as I have already explained, is that psychotherapy is not a procedure wherein the therapist performs an exact and prescribed operation. Since it is as much an art as a science, it is highly dependent not only upon the qualities of the two individuals involved, but on the combination of their two separate personalities.

Geraldine was a psychologist, whose unsuccessful treatment with me I discuss in chapter 10. She had had two unsatisfactory attempts at psychotherapy before she came to me and so I was most reluctant to accept the fact that we could not work together successfully. Nonetheless, from the beginning there was considerable friction between us which never entirely disappeared. She and I had quite different views as to how I should deal with her. She wanted me to be much more "classical," saying less, letting her project more onto me. I felt that it was essential to be active in confronting her with how she dealt with me and how it affected me. We had some months of modest achievement, but in the end, not surprisingly, it did not work. The failure was due to differences in who we were and what we wanted the treatment to be, and we never resolved those differences.

On the other hand, Teresa (chapter 2) was not very well matched with her therapist. But while both realized that she had not achieved the best result of which she was capable, they were able to compromise sufficiently to get a satisfactory result.

If it is true, as I believe, that the two parties should match each other well, then one might expect that therapists would have some formal way of testing for a good fit and, thence, making the best possible referrals. Unfortunately, no tests have been devised to identify potential partners for marriage and by the same token, there is no formal way to predict the outcome of matching patient and therapist. Such choices are best made by use of common judgment, based both upon life experience and upon paying serious attention to one's own instinctive reactions.

A patient, when I suggest a therapist for him to approach, will often ask me: "How will I know if I have found a person with whom I can work, and how long should I persevere if it does not seem to be going well?" My usual answer is: "If your initial feeling is positive there is a good chance that things will work out well between you, but if you have negative feelings you should pay attention to them. Unless there is a very good reason to discontinue after the first visit you should try again, at least once, and if you are still uncertain, for a few weeks. But do not force yourself to continue against strong inner negative feelings. Such feelings indicate that in all likelihood you have important reservations about the therapist as a person and those reservations are unlikely to disappear." Some therapists have the opposite point of view to the one I have expressed. They see all problems between therapist and patient as residing in the latter. Any misgivings on the part of the patient as to the rightness of the match are labeled "resistances" and he is told that he should continue in the therapeutic situation striving to get past such "resistance."

Of course, at times resistance does arise within all patients, and for one clear and valid reason. In order to avoid the pain and discomfort which is caused by the recognition of the truth, the patient tends to resist the therapy itself. However, there are often other compelling and important reasons for a patient's reluctance to continue with treatment and these should be respected by the therapist.

Eleanor was given the name of an experienced psychotherapist because she wanted help with the depressive feelings that kept assailing her. Within the first week she experienced difficulty in talking to the therapist; this was not typical of her, as she was naturally a loquacious person. As she struggled with her inability to express herself the therapist kept saying again and again: "You are resisting, why are you resisting?" The words had no meaning to her. All she knew was that she had little or nothing to say. After a month of treatment she did not keep an appointment, then telephoned to say that she would not be back. The therapeutic process had never gotten off the ground.

The principal problem in this instance was that the patient felt, from the beginning, that the therapist was not aware of her as a person. The therapy was perceived by the therapist in a very mechanistic way: there was a job to be done which he as a trained practitioner was equipped to do, so any difficulties in the carrying out of this operation must be due to balking or "resistance" on the part of the patient.

Eleanor was as strongly motivated toward being helped as are most of those patients who make a success of therapy. She had a few reservations but they were not so great that a way could not have been found around them. She needed time to get going, and supportive assistance from the therapist to help her understand what was expected of her. The repeated accusation that she was "resisting" was felt by her as what indeed it was—an attack of unjustified criticism. In the wake of such criticism, she became increasingly unable to expose her feelings until finally she was forced to terminate the therapy.

Eleanor never went to another therapist, since that experience was so bad that she doubted that she could be helped. She has lived for twenty years with problems within her personality which were treatable. Life would have been considerably better for her had that one experience with therapy been different.

Jerome was referred for treatment when he was seventeen years of age. He was moderately rebellious, and his well-to-do parents could not accept the fact that he would not apply himself at school. He spent three years in therapy with a child psychiatrist, and described the process as follows:

"I didn't like him the day I met him, and that never really changed. He told me early on that my problem was that I wasn't very smart, and he took my behavior, my school record, as well as psychological tests to prove that, but I knew that that was not the problem. It is true that I am not a good student. But I always felt within myself that I was capable of doing well at something, and that has been proven by my work history in the past few years. I was aware that he held an unduly negative view of me, which I could do nothing to change."

I asked Jerome some years later, when he was seeking another therapist, why he had persevered so long with treatment which had gone so badly.

"Well," he said, "my father had always tried to do his best for me and he was convinced that my therapist was first class. I was a troubled boy with little confidence in myself. I kept thinking that the fault must lie with me, not with my therapist, and yet I knew that he was wrong in holding such a prejudiced view of me. I was so

bogged down by a general feeling of hopelessness about my life, that I did not have the strength or courage to fight his negative attitude or even to turn away from it. So I just put up with it."

Despite his poor relationship with the therapist, Jerome did get something from the treatment, since it was his first opportunity to talk about himself to an experienced person. The therapy was not as helpful as it might have been but it did allow him to grow enough eventually to break off the relationship. After a few years without treatment, he recognized that there was still a great deal that he needed help to accomplish. He sought a consultation with me and I referred him to another therapist with whom, from the beginning, he felt comfortable. Because of his positive feelings, Jerome achieved much more with the second therapist than he would ever have done with the first.

The examples I have given thus far illustrate a poor match. In Eleanor's case it was fortunate that she recognized, almost immediately, that something was wrong and discontinued her therapy, but Jerome did not have enough self-confidence to stop his treatment, so he let it go on for a few years.

In some instances the fit is particularly good and a bond is quickly established between the two people. The patient likes and is ready to trust the therapist who in turn is aware of this and expects to be able to be of some help. This creates a climate for the therapy in which a great deal can be accomplished. When I say that trust on the patient's part exists early on, I refer to an instinctive trust not a deep trust, for this latter will only develop in time, after he has experienced, again and again, that the therapist has his interests at heart and strives to help him grow. As for the therapist, he is attracted to such a patient from the beginning and has a sense that the potential exists for a good relationship between them. As the weeks, months and perhaps years of treatment unfold he experiences the pleasure that comes from working hard at a creative and difficult task, knowing that with a good match he can do his most productive work.

Psychotherapy is work and it is not easy. It should not be principally painful, though it needs to be painful at times. In the well-matched therapeutic pair there is a kind of teamwork which both participants perceive in a very positive way. The initial impression, on the part of both therapist and patient, that they will get along well is based largely on intuition, but as the therapy proceeds they will discover more fully how they suit one another: in temperament, in attitudes, in values, or in character.

Over the years this has happened to me with certain patients, one of the first of whom was Charles. The day we met for our initial consultation we were both aware of this. He spilled out his story with very little help needed from me. We both had a similar sense of humor, so that even though he had come in pain, there were several times on that occasion when we laughed wrily or smiled together. His mind moved nimbly through his problems and when I responded with some opinions about him, he took them up quickly and openly.

We worked together in psychotherapy for a few years. It was easy for both of us. We worked as a team. There was little conflict and much was accomplished. I had a sense of exhilaration when I realized, early in our work together, how well we suited each other.

During our final session Charles said:

"It has been so easy for me. I thought it was supposed to be hard."

"It was so easy for me," I replied, "that it often felt wrong accepting payment from you."

He laughed. "Does it usually happen this way?"

"No, but when it does it is a pleasure and we were able to move quickly, since there was no struggle with each other, only with the task."

*We shared our feelings of pleasure that the work had been success-
ful. Occasionally he calls me up to say hello. We both feel fortunate
that, when he needed help, he found his way to me.*

It sometimes occurs that the fit between therapist and patient is so good that the potential for a real and deep friendship
resides within the therapeutic relationship. That such a
friendship can develop has to be considered a fortunate coincidence, similar to that which exists when two strangers meet
and in time become friends. The prime purpose of the therapy, to foster the growth and development of the patient, does
not change as long as the treatment continues, but sometimes
the difficult and productive work of therapy helps develop
other satisfactions for the two people involved. In such cases
the friendship which began in the course of psychotherapy
will then have a life of its own. Jeanne Lampl-de Groot commented on this question in an article looking back over fifty
years of the practice of psychoanalysis, as follows:

> In later times a real friendship with a few of my former analy-
> sands . . . also came into existence, although I am quite aware
> of the fact that such a relationship is possible and rewarding
> with only a few. One important precondition is the resolution of
> transference and countertransference to such a degree that ideal-
> ization and competitive hostility are sufficiently conquered by
> both the analysand and the analyst. In addition certain char-
> acter traits, a like-mindedness, a not too different outlook on
> life, among others, are necessary for the formation of a "real
> friendship." One can analyze persons of a quite dissimilar back-
> ground and philosophy of life but a lasting friendship does not
> come into being in such circumstances.

Although occasionally, after the therapy has ended, the
former patient and therapist will continue to have a place

within each other's lives, often this will not be the case and they will rarely if ever see one another. Even then the feelings of friendship will remain alive in the two people and will be perceived by them both, with gratitude, as an unexpected but most welcome by-product of the successful therapy.

Louise, a writer, had been in psychotherapy with me, once a week, for three years. Since that time she has called and arranged to see me, usually about once a year. Recently she wrote me, as I was out of town for some months, to bring me up-to-date, and she commented on this question of friendship between patient and therapist:

"I often feel fortunate that at a point when my life seemed to be closing in on me, the therapist I found was right for me and I don't doubt that there have been ripple effects in countless directions. I also feel grateful that I made a friend in that arduous search, a friend albeit different from others, but then what two friendships are the same? And don't all of them have contexts of one kind or another? . . ."

This was Louise's way of expressing her gratitude for the feelings of friendship, which remain with both of us, following the work we did together.

4

"THERE IS A TIDE
IN THE AFFAIRS OF MEN"
The World in Which the Therapy Occurs

INDIVIDUAL psychotherapy is so all-consuming a process that the error is often made of reacting to it as though it took place within a vacuum. Of course it does not. In order to be able more clearly to identify those factors in the patient's life that derive from within himself, psychoanalysts have tried to set aside the external influences, and concentrate as much as possible on the patient's internal world.

In Freud's time, psychoanalysis was of brief duration. A patient might be seen for a few weeks, or a few months. It was the exception for someone to be treated continually over a period of years. At that time treatment was aimed at specific symptoms. In more recent times the therapist's aim has been to include *all* aspects of the patient's personality, so that the duration of treatment has been much longer. (Sometimes this gets out of hand, with endless treatment, which has no discernible effect.) Because the treatment was shorter, the early analysts were able to suggest to their patients that important life changes should be avoided during the course of the analysis. It is possible to take this position during an analysis which lasts for a year. It is indefensible to do so during therapy that extends over a number of years, since basic steps such as career choice, marriage, having children, and so on must be taken when time and opportunity are propitious, not at some artificial moment indicated by the termination of treatment.

When the patient is faced with making major choices it is the therapist's responsibility to examine them with him in therapy. The purpose of such examination is for both parties to learn what feelings are attached to the making of each decision, and what issues are at stake. This will help the patient to increase his ability to make choices that will be better rather than worse for him.

George was in analysis several hours a week for a period of years. In the early months it became clear that he had two divergent points of view operating inside himself. On the one hand, because of attitudes in his family which had existed for at least the three generations he had known, he was highly impressed with ambitious, wealthy, "successful" people, and, being well endowed himself, felt driven to become and to marry such a person. On the other hand, there was a down-to-earth, sensible part of himself which recognized the danger in such goals. His father had been a kind, family-oriented man, hardworking and unsophisticated. The patient had a deep identification as well with these qualities, which were evident in the personality of a young woman he met while in the first year of analysis. She was a quiet person who would not, at first meeting, catch anyone's attention. She was modest, in those days self-effacing to a fault. She took a rather benign view of the patient's ambitious and wealthy relatives, and was not much impressed by those whom he admired and envied. Nor was she excited by the prospect of being married to a man who might become rich or famous or both. Her background was ordinary, which meant that his family would be disappointed, and show it, should he select such a mate. One of the early struggles in the analysis for the patient was whether or not he should marry this woman. The conflict within him caused him much pain, but in the end he decided in favor of the more simple part of himself and they were married.

George, with the analyst, discovered in treatment that she had certain character traits which were of great importance to him. These included loyalty, simplicity, and unpretentiousness. Fortunately, the analyst felt it was essential to pay attention to such matters and supported him in his decision.

It would be fair to say that, had George not been in analysis at the time he met his future wife, he would have had much more difficulty over the decision to marry her. But it would be naive and incorrect to ignore, in all the years which followed, the profound effect that the choice of that partner had upon him.

In the first place, the analysis became easier for the patient, and for the analyst, because of her influence. The patient's more neurotic attitudes, rather than being magnified by the self-centered or highly intellectual woman he might have married, were toned down and neutralized by her common sense and down-to-earth approach. George was repeatedly surprised in the early years at how she could understand their life together in the most simple terms. Her plain and insightful outlook helped to reinforce the healthier attitudes within himself. This was of enormous importance to him, and indirectly to his analysis.

Individual psychotherapists differ greatly in terms of the position that they adopt vis à vis the patient's life outside the therapy. The classical view might be presented by a psychoanalyst in this way:

"Do not look at what is around you, look at what is inside you. I am not interested in your spouse, your friends, your children, I am interested in you. It is only your reactions and your viewpoint which are important to your analysis. When you become preoccupied with the effect something or someone around you has upon

you, it is a diversion from the central theme, evidence of resistance against discovering the truth, within you, which we seek."

A clear example of this attitude is the following:

Sheldon is a social worker who had been in psychoanalysis for about two years. His wife fell ill and died after several months of illness. In the months that followed, most of the time in the analysis was taken up with his talking about his wife, what she had meant to him, how he missed her. One day the analyst said to him: "All you have been talking about is your wife. There is no room in your life for analysis now." The analyst terminated the analysis. This step was grossly unfair. What Sheldon was engaged in was a normal, expected process of mourning. The analyst was unprepared to deal with the patient's real-life situation and real feelings and ended treatment just when it could have been most valuable. Fortunately, Sheldon changed to another analyst who offered him the opportunity of carrying on the process of mourning within the analysis.

Some therapists will have nothing to do with anyone connected to the patient. They will not speak on the telephone to a relative and are reluctant to send information to referring doctors or hospitals involved in the patient's care. This is an extreme position which will not achieve the best results. It came about in an attempt to create "a pure field" for the examination of the patient; but when the therapist fails to deal with the patient's world it is unlikely that he will be able to see him realistically. In addition, family members, not surprisingly, resent being shut out of the treatment process. To exclude those who are important to the patient, tends to encourage the view that psychotherapy is some mystical experience that nobody can understand. Therapists who have come to realize that such a position is harmful to the patient, have developed a treatment which includes all members of the family, in family therapy. Although this has been an important step forward, it too is sometimes carried to an extreme wherein the therapist refuses to treat *anybody* unless *everybody* in the family participates.

There are no rules to dictate how the therapist should behave in this matter of meeting people other than the patient. Sometimes, but not always, it is essential for the therapist to meet the spouse, child, friend, or employer of the patient. At other times the therapist may be asked by the patient to see someone so that he can understand them more clearly. It is best that the therapist be flexible and arrange whatever meetings seem useful in his task of helping the patient.

When someone is in therapy for a significant length of time, he will not be exactly the same person when the therapy ends as he was when it started. This may seem obvious, but too often when therapists discuss patients they ignore the fact that over a period of several years the patient has been subjected to different influences, has sustained many losses, and has achieved some goals, all of which have caused him to change.

It is not only the changes in the patient's life which will influence the course of the therapy. A therapist who is single and just starting up a practice when treatment begins is not the same as the therapist who ends the treatment married and the parent of two children. He will have learned from the stresses to which he has been subjected, and one of the changes will be that he feels more able to discuss with the patient the role of spouse or parent. Also, he may become less blaming of the patient's parents. This is not to say that a therapist needs to have undergone all the patient's experiences in order to help him. It is possible for an inexperienced therapist to understand a patient and to do good work for him. But the experienced therapist is in an even better position to know, with some depth and hence fuller understanding, what the patient means about how he feels.

One day, when I had been in practice only a few years, I opened the door of my waiting room. There sat a sixty-year-old gentleman whom I was to see in consultation for the first time. His face fell.

"How do you do, I'm Dr. Greben. Won't you come in?" He took a seat and I said: "You looked very surprised when you saw me."

"I was," he replied.

"In what way?"

"You don't look the way I imagined you would."

"You mean that I look younger than you expected?"

"That's right."

"What had you pictured?"

"Someone older, probably with a beard, and gray hair."

"More like Sigmund Freud?" I smiled.

"Yes."

"Why would my looking so young worry you?"

"Well, I don't feel you could understand me. You are too young to have been where I have been, or to have encountered the problems I have faced."

"You are right. Still, a doctor learns about life in many ways. Certainly his own life helps him. Books help a bit, but not a lot. He should learn a lot from his patients."

"That makes sense."

"The main thing is, I'm going to have to learn about you from you. We shall see whether or not I can understand what you tell me. Now, let me begin by asking you some questions."

It has often happened, after treatment that has lasted for years, that a patient will tell me how different I am from when the therapy began. A small part of the observation may not be correct; for the patient may so have changed in the course of the therapy that even if I were exactly the same, he would perceive me differently and, in all likelihood, much more accurately. But by far the largest part of the patient's observation is correct, and I acknowledge this to him. Usually we are both amused by the fact that as I became more experienced I became more helpful to him. In most instances the patient, if his experience in therapy has been generally positive, will smile and forgive me for the fact that I was less use to him early in the therapy. Occasionally, the patient feels cheated by my earlier inexperienced efforts. Ordinarily we conclude together that, unavoidably, one has to survive the less-than-perfect therapist. Some patients can see that part of how the therapist has grown and improved has been through the experience he has had in treating them. In that case, the patient may be pleased that he has unwittingly been his therapist's teacher.

Zelda was my first supervised psychoanalytic patient. Because I was training to be a psychoanalyst, and her treatment was part of that process, she had to be seen by a senior analyst before I could take her on. Zelda did not seem concerned about this, in part because she knew that I was already an experienced psychotherapist before deciding to train as an analyst.

There was a period of several years, after the psychoanalysis had been terminated, when Zelda and I did not see each other. She had left the treatment feeling markedly improved, had married, and had changed the course of her life vocationally. Overall, she was pleased with what the two of us had accomplished. One day Zelda called and asked to see me. Things were going well and she wanted to bring me up-to-date. We met for an hour. We were both very pleased to meet again.

"It's great to see you again," she said.

"It's great to see you."

"I didn't have any problem to discuss. I just thought it had been a long time, and that I'd like to see you and bring you up-to-date."

"Good." She told me the main things that had happened since we last met. Then she asked: "And what is new with you?"

I was pleasantly surprised. It was the first time she had put such a question to me. I told her generally about the main aspects of my life at that time. Then I said: "And I am currently writing a book about psychotherapy."

"That's wonderful. What will it include?" I told her.

"If you agree, I would like to use two of those poems you gave me for a chapter on humor."

"That's fine. I would be very pleased if you would."

In the course of this discussion it came out that her psychoanalysis had been the first I had conducted. She was filled with pleasure at this discovery. Part of this was that it gave her a sense of having been and still being special to me, and special in a way she had not known about. This was indeed the reality. Another part of it was the pleasure at realizing that she had made, without her knowledge, a significant contribution toward my development as a therapist: since she had been my first patient in psychoanalysis, it was with her that I learned that I could be a psychoanalyst. This, too, was a reality. She was able to see how I had changed over the course of her treatment and also over the subsequent years. All of this gave her a sense of pleasure and pride, and was a further factor in her being able to feel more adult in relation to me.

There is another way in which psychotherapy and the patient's outside realities are closely related. Shakespeare said: "There is a tide in the affairs of men . . ." and much depends upon how we address that tide. A great deal of what happens to bring change for the better through psychotherapy arises out of the patient's improved capacity to ride favorable tides. George's marriage was an example of this. The therapist cannot create opportunities which would benefit the patient, but he can be highly instrumental in helping the patient take full advantage of those opportunities which do occur. As we have seen, both psychotherapist and patient need to address the question of whether or not people from the patient's life should meet the therapist. The advantage of not doing so is that the patient will know that the therapist has only heard his point of view and has not been influenced by another opinion. This can lead to the development of trust on the patient's part. The disadvantage is that the therapist runs the risk of having a one-sided view of the people in the patient's world, and to be fair in this respect is a serious challenge to him. How accurate was Portnoy's complaint about his mother? How possible would it have been for Portnoy's analyst not to be unduly prejudiced against her? Often a patient, especially one who is fair-minded, or who easily feels guilt, says: "How do you know that what I tell you is true? After all, it is only my point of view, and I know that not everyone would agree with it."

I usually reply: "I have ample evidence that you are a fair person. In fact, I always notice how you bend over backwards to protect the image of your father. Also, when someone speaks at such length about his life, if there are inconsistencies, then in time they show up. In addition, I have heard a lot about your friends, who are people of integrity, and it is clear that they think a good deal of you and trust you." On the other hand, when I am uncertain that I am getting a true picture and the patient asks me that question, I might say: "Sometimes I do have serious doubts about the views you express to me. Some inconsistencies, which I have pointed out to you, worry me. You should know that I have doubts about whether I can always believe what you tell me."

When the patient's point of view is skewed by the strongest of feelings, as Portnoy's might very well have been, the therapist may have the feeling that he is not hearing the truth. In some instances he will want to meet the person concerned in order to check out the patient's view against that person's view. Of course, this can only be done with the patient's knowledge and consent. With a patient who too easily takes offense or feels slighted, the therapist might propose that the patient be present when such a meeting takes place.

In summary, the world in which the therapy occurs is always important and must be perceived with reasonable accuracy by the therapist. That world may have a profound effect, either positive or negative, upon the course of therapy. The therapist needs to understand not only the patient's inner world, but the world around him. Then he can help the patient to see more clearly what surrounds him and how he can deal with it more effectively.

LISTENING WITH TWO EARS: THE MUSIC BEHIND THE WORDS

Theodore Reik entitled his book about psychoanalysis, *Listening with the Third Ear*. In it he suggests that we should try to hear the music behind the words. Before we can do that, however, we have to be able to listen with the two ears with which we were born. The patient's private world is often surrounded by an impregnable wall. If the therapist is ever to be allowed to enter, he must first have demonstrated that he is a careful and interested listener. Listening isn't easy; that is, really listening. Everyone knows that the first requirement of a psychotherapist is to listen. But it is probably commonly imagined that listening is easier than it is.

The first connection between people, that is between mother and fetus, is through a deeply shared physical experience. The mother feeds and shelters her baby through her circulatory system which is in touch with his. After birth, the next connection between people is also physical: the infant is *held* in his mother's arms. Whereas we must forever give up the first arrangement, people of all ages seek something close to the second. They need touching and caressing either in a truly intimate way or more casually as with a simple pat on the back.

People can also connect with each other through silence or with subtle gestures but in psychotherapy, as in most human contacts, speech is the principal means of communication. For the patient, speaking is difficult because the more he reveals of himself the more he risks being hurt. For the therapist, learning how to listen is one of the greatest demands placed upon him.

In life very few people listen; to confirm this, the reader only has to observe his friends, colleagues, or relatives. If you watch carefully those to whom you are speaking, you will often notice that they do not give you their full attention. Their eyes glaze over, their glance wanders, they become restless, and they interrupt. They can hardly wait to speak about whatever pertains to themselves.

Much conversation would not take place if we were not so insistent on having an opportunity to talk. The person who can manage to remain silent will be allowed and even encouraged to do so. We are not free to listen to him because we are so pressed to speak and to be heard ourselves. Our need to express our ideas and our feelings is not the only reason for this. There is an additional pressure which stems from the fact that we are seldom really heard, for our words fall on deaf ears.

Why is it that people can so rarely listen? In part it is because we have not been taught to do so. We have neither been instructed in the value of listening to others, nor have we had the experience of someone carefully and caringly listening to us. This latter would be the best way to learn. However, probably the most important reason is that should we really listen we may be hurt by what is said. Unfortunately, this is a problem which exists in some therapists, who cannot tolerate hearing some of what the patient thinks and feels.

The listener may also be hurt through the very fact that he is listening, not speaking; in other words he is giving, not receiving. His own strong need to receive makes it hard for him to tolerate the one who speaks. By listening to him he is creating a better situation for the speaker than for himself, which makes him envious. The person who is listening may also compare himself to the one who is speaking, and the comparison may be painful; or what he is hearing may be threatening to him, thus stimulating feelings of apprehension or anxiety.

Psychotherapists are products of their environments. They are developed out of their own societies. So they also tend to suffer from all I have described. Of course, those who become psychotherapists are not a randomly selected sample from the general population. To begin with, they value words and communication and so they have been attracted to such a profession. Many are not, in their personal lives, very successful at communicating with others, so their choice of this vocation may be partly governed by an unconscious wish to have this special way of being close to people.

Still, when psychotherapists are trained, they have to be taught to listen, and this means that most of them have to overcome decades of not listening. As a teacher of psychiatric residents I have found that most of them are readily able to learn to *listen*. What is more difficult is to learn to *hear*. In order to do that the psychotherapist must deal with the problems I have mentioned that arise within the person who really hears. If they feel envy, then they must understand and work with some of their inner tendencies toward being envious. This may, for example, be a special problem in the treatment of a powerful, rich, or gifted person. If anxiety is the troublesome emotion experienced, then they must come to know more about themselves, so as to recognize some of the sources of that anxiety.

I have said that most psychotherapists do indeed learn to listen during the course of their work. In spite of any difficulty they may have in communicating in their social lives, they are good at listening to their patients and can be of great help to them.

The patient arrives in therapy hungry to be heard. He has to overcome his reluctance to speak, and in the company of a competent therapist he will gradually do so. He will be greatly relieved by the act of speaking, even before the therapist has said anything. When in therapy, a patient will ordinarily assume that he is well understood, even by the silent therapist who only responds with monosyllables. That assumption, even if it is incorrect, is in itself therapeutic. If he feels that he is in a milieu which is receptive and understanding he will improve.

The songwriter in Neil Simon's musical, *They're Playing Our Song*, has taken this situation one step further. Having already had years of psychoanalysis, he has concluded that the analyst is not essential to the process. And so twice weekly he lies on a couch and for an hour talks about and to himself. He finds himself a receptive and understanding audience. And, even more, he finds the process helpful, that is therapeutic. The playwright has made a serious comment with some good humor and some irony.

If the therapist *is* in fact receptive and *does* understand the patient, then that is the best possible arrangement. It is one in which the patient will be able to grow or recover as fully as possible and the therapy will be successful. The wish to be listened to and to be heard is universal and lifelong. When people are offered this opportunity, they flourish, when they are not, they suffer profoundly.

Journalist Francis X. Clines accompanied Iris Schwartz, a social worker from the Mid-Bronx Senior Citizens Council, on her rounds one day. He observed: "Feeding them is one thing . . . But talking to them—ah, there's a luxury for the isolated old people that's at least as savory as the hot food too many of the bewildered loners barely poke at. . . . Mid-Bronx needs volunteers to talk to old people—an act of total charity, because the day has not yet been reached when the Government will pay people to talk to one another. . . . [One old woman] is smiling as she talks . . . She enjoys seeing Iris listen, and, after almost a century of life, she seems to value talk as much as hot food."

The patient, like these old people and all other human beings, longs to be understood. He does not want to be known only by his overt and sometimes defensive behavior. He wants the therapist to hear "the music behind the words." To offer someone such understanding is to present him with a gift of great value.

Marie, to whom I have previously referred, was treated by me once a week over a period of several years. She worked in a profession which required her to deal with clients in a helping capacity. She did this skillfully and effectively. When she came to psychotherapy she'd already had a previous, unsuccessful period of treatment. She was in her early thirties and desperately unhappy. She had often contemplated suicide. The most striking quality of her life was its emptiness and the absence of any pleasure.

"Can you tell me why you called me?"

"I am just miserable. I feel wretched. I am alienated from everybody around me. No one cares for me—they all think I'm a half-crazy old maid." She did not look directly at me during that first interview. Her head hung down. But I saw that she kept darting glances at me, checking me over, seeing whether I was what she had been seeking. She seemed to be locked up inside herself, yet although she tried to hide it, was hyperalert to all that was going on around her.

"What is crazy about you?"

"I look crazy. I stumble over myself whenever I try to do anything. My low class way of speaking betrays where I was born: it makes people think that I am both uneducated and stupid."

"You sound as though you are neither." She looked directly at me for a moment. The suggestion of a smile touched her face.

Marie suffered from chronically debilitating anxiety. She could hardly sit still. She was under tremendous pressure to speak, pouring out words of anxiety and loneliness. She spoke much but said little. She was odd in many ways. She had been raised in Europe and had been fundamentally neglected by her parents. The marked poverty of her family all through her life had been a source of painful humiliation. She had, when she first came, an unusual, almost bizarre appearance. She seemed constantly in a frenzy. Her odd manner and strange behavior could easily have led a therapist to feel repelled, both by her differentness and by the magnitude of the task of helping her to improve. Everything pointed against her being able to change. Marie came to therapy regularly, always on time. She had not had, nor did she expect to have, the experience of being listened to and taken seriously. In the therapeutic session, she often talked nonstop. It was only possible for her to come once a week, and there was infinitely more to be said than could be expressed in this brief time. As do many patients, she augmented the sessions by thinking and "talking" to me in her own mind between sessions. Even this did not suffice. She asked whether she could write letters to me between visits. I agreed that she could do so.

Each week one, two or even three letters would arrive by mail. Some were as short as a page or two. Others covered twenty or thirty pages. The understanding was that I would read them all if I possibly could but, should that not be possible, I would do so eventually.

"I sent you four letters this week."

"Yes. I received them all." She paused, looked as if she were going to speak, then fell silent.

"What were you beginning to say?"

"Is it okay that I send you all that?"

I smiled. "It's okay. I'm managing."

Then she smiled. "I'm glad you can joke about it. Sometimes it pours out of me as if there is no bottom to the cesspool I feel inside of me. I don't know where it all comes from. I'm afraid sometimes that you'll drown in it."

"I won't. But you almost have. Your analogy is a good one. You were dying to share all of those feelings with someone. When it became possible, a tap was opened. It will run fast for a while."

"I hope I don't have to stop it."

"You don't have to."

A casual observer would have seen little change in Marie over the years. Perhaps she would have appeared moderately less frantic, perhaps not. But within herself she felt very powerfully influenced by the experience of the therapy.

During the course of the treatment and in the years that have followed, in her own estimation Marie has changed enormously. When asked, years after therapy had ended, to comment on what had happened in treatment, she wrote about many of the influences which had been helpful to her. She summed up her view of the experience by saying: "One thing is certain—I *totally* changed."

Some of what Marie wrote is relevant to our present area of concern, namely, being listened to, and the effects which this can have upon people. In part she wrote as follows:

"I was so tired of the problems myself, I expected the therapist to become bored, impatient, perhaps angry, early on. He didn't and I began to see my difficulties as real and something I had to work on hard. I had been labeled as a hysteric, and I'd begun to think of myself as playacting. For the first time, the therapist assured me I wasn't basically acting, and I did have real difficulties. And that problem solving was possible, although long term. Within the sec-

ond interview, the therapist started to move in on this 'acting' defense and I had to start feeling again, which I did not want to do—too painful . . .

"It was set down plainly that the sessions were work. This I liked. I was being taken seriously. I wasn't beating at a brick wall. I think from that time, suicide was not likely—what was the point of it any more? Someone had heard the cries and responded, promptly and efficiently. . . .

"Plain words were used from the beginning. We took specters out of the closet and looked at them. The therapist was not upset, or afraid, even if I was. I had to acknowledge the problems at first; then, as I began to be more assured, confident in the therapist, I wanted to think about them, to talk them over.

"In the first session, the businesslike, matter-of-fact attitude of the therapist, plus his personal appearance, his office set-up, and what I had already dug up about him, led me to form a very favorable impression . . . At that point I started to talk about things that weren't part of the polite world, to test the response. As I've said, the response was not what was anticipated, and that meant I had to go on in therapy . . . For literally years, I was so frightened I had trouble talking. To this day I'm not sure why I was so terror-stricken. But this I brought into the therapeutic situation, and the therapist realized it, and didn't reprimand me. Quietly he tried to find ways around the problem. I think his attitude helped me tremendously. I knew he was helping me to find my own answers, even if I had no idea of the source of the problem. The therapist became the only source of security I had, or had known. I was never 'put-down.' There was no hint of sarcasm, ridicule, impatience, or of a power-play . . .

"I felt that nonverbal communication between us was excellent, and I still do not know how the therapist accomplished this, but it happened . . .

"Although I was sure it was a burden (and I wondered what he'd do about it), being allowed to write when I could not talk was a tremendous help to me . . .

"*The sessions gave an incredible feeling of peace and calm (eventually, not at first). This was overwhelmingly important to me. I would have paid to have the privilege of sitting in companionate calm with the therapist, because this was nonexistent in the rest of my life. It seemed as though we were out of human time during the sessions; as though when I walked through the door something happened. I had walked into reality . . .*

"*I think the therapist's nonverbal attitude was the most important thing here—decisions were mine, but he was behind me. I felt that if anything was going really awry, I could turn to him, or I'd be told . . .*

"*It was a sort of bonding experience, because it was intensely personal, letting the therapist in to a very private world. Latterly, there was literally nothing I couldn't have told the therapist if I'd had the chance. The therapist let it be known that it was okay to be me—but that therapy was a change process.*"

Marie developed very slowly from a terrified, pressured woman, constantly beset by anxiety and obsession, to an effective strong leader in her work. Her appearance changed markedly; her expression was open. She looked directly at the person she spoke to, and often spoke challengingly. The apologetic aspect of her personality changed. She now gave the appearance of being a vigorous, aggressive, and intelligent woman. She had always done well with her clients, because of her high intelligence, warm-hearted understanding of pain and deprivation, and because of her iron determination. Therapy gave her the opportunity of being heard, of being free to explore who she was and discover who she could ultimately be. In her own view, the changes were "total," and it all began with listening and hearing.

5

FACING A HOST OF PAINFUL TRUTHS
Insight

What is the end of study? let me know.
Why, that to know which else we should not know.
Things hid and barr'd, you mean, from common sense?
Ay, that is study's gold-like recompense.

Love's Labours Lost
WILLIAM SHAKESPEARE

IT HELPS in more than one way to understand oneself and one's world. Most people who become patients suffer without knowing why. They are deprived in certain ways and suffer the pain of those deprivations. This leads to symptoms of many kinds. The symptoms, in turn, lead to fear and upset because of the many terrors which are unknown. A sense of helplessness arises out of not knowing what is happening to them, and as a result, what might happen in the future. Many upsets, which psychiatrists will label as neuroses, or psychoses, or character disorders, are at their worst caused by a fear of the unknown. Very frequently the gravest aspect of phobias, for example the fear of going into open places (agoraphobia) or the fear of being closed in or stifled (claustrophobia) is the terror that some unknown thing will befall one. Many patients with such problems are afraid that they will drop dead. They do not understand why their heart races or skips beats, why they overbreathe, why they feel dizzy or light-headed, or weak and enervated. Understanding diminishes or eliminates fear.

Marjorie was referred to me by her family doctor. She was a housewife with three small children, and was sent to see me because she had complained to her doctor of an inability to enjoy sex. This was the key which gave her entry into psycho-therapy. In fact, it was one of the least of her problems.

Marjorie, as I later learned, was an alcoholic. She was chronically depressed. I treated this latter symptom with medication, and within the first year of our treatment she had become dependent upon several of them. Through the early years of her treatment the severity of her illness became in-creasingly apparent. On several occasions it was necessary to admit her to a psychiatric hospital for a few weeks or a few months, because she had become psychotic, and was in danger of harming herself or her children. Hospital care pro-vided safety and the fuller use of medical treatments, and when she was sufficiently improved she would always return to outpatient psychotherapy.

After five years of once-a-week psychotherapy she was stronger. She stopped drinking, the drug dependence was brought under control, the terrible depressions began to di-minish in intensity and duration, but she still had grave prob-lems. I wondered at that stage how much Marjorie could ac-complish. She had been ill for many years and there was good reason to fear that she might not recover. However, I was encouraged by a number of factors. She was intelligent and hard working in the therapy, wanting, even intending, to make a success of it. She had an almost photographic capacity to remember events and feelings, so that she was able to recapture a great deal from her early years. Whereas she had not been "psychologically minded" when she came, she had a natural intuitive understanding of those insights which began to emerge in the treatment. Finally, she did not flinch in the face of the pain which came with understanding, but persevered in her attempt to face the truth of her life. All of these factors made me decide that there was much more that she could accomplish through further psychotherapy.

Marjorie took many new steps over the years. She went back to complete her university training, took further education which allowed her to enter a profession and, in her forties, began a new career. She now works full time at a challenging job in which she helps others who are, as she had been, disadvantaged.

Marjorie is a most direct and honest person. Unlike many people, she made full use, in therapy, of her intelligence and retentive memory. She struggled her way through terrible memories of her early and later years, facing a host of painful truths. The essence of these truths was that those who had reared her and those who had been close to her in adult life had used and exploited her cruelly. Her contribution, from the beginning, had been to avoid seeing this because she did not want to face how disappointing these people were to her. As she grew up she continued to form relationships with people who would neglect or even torture her. But her own lack of self-esteem made her always find herself at fault.

Marjorie's mother was psychotic, although she was never treated, either in or outside of a hospital. She was insanely jealous of her daughter, a young, gifted, and ingenuous girl, and tried to keep her in her place by domineering, intimidating, and shaming her. She took sadistic pleasure in depriving her of anything which might please her, and throughout her life was her cruel tormentor both physically and emotionally. I had many occasions to wonder why Marjorie had not developed a chronic psychosis, as had her mother. The answer lay, I believe, in two main factors. The first was her unusually generous constitutional endowment, to which I have already referred. The second was the fact that a couple of very good and caring people had loved her during early life: first, her father, who had died suddenly in her early years; and second, an aunt with whom she had lived as a very young child. These good experiences had been kept alive within her so that, along with her recovery of the terrible memories of her abuse and neglect, she also uncovered the warmth and love and affection of those two very special people.

Marjorie's view of the people in her world, including herself, is now clear and uncluttered. She harbors no illusions about the goodness or worth of those who happen to be related to her, or who expect to be considered her friend. She is not unhappy or depressed about how she sees people to be, but realistic and interested. She has become moderately cynical, but not the least bitter. Anger, depression, and fear no longer overwhelm her. She is neither boastful nor self-effacing, but has a quiet confidence in her own judgment, her own ideas, and her own worth. Her conviction is extremely strong, without arrogance. Her self-confidence has, as far as I can detect, no derogation of anyone else included in it.

Because she has changed so much over the years, I have often used Marjorie as someone who could help me understand what it is about psychotherapy that can lead to change. In fact she will agree, from time to time, to speak with a psychiatric resident or medical student who wants to understand more about this question.

When I was writing this description I called Marjorie to have her opinion on this matter.

"Would you tell me in one brief sentence what helped you?" I asked. She paused for a moment. I had called her at work, and she had to adjust the focus of her thinking.

"You always treated me with respect," she replied. She hesitated. "No, that isn't exactly it. In fact, you actually did respect me."

"I see. What else has been important?"

"Understanding is also very important—the insight. With what I have learned I can pretty well hope to maintain my present state for as long as I live. Insight wasn't important in the beginning; change is very gradual in coming. The important thing is that I can be an independent person. The insight is most connected to my peace of mind, within myself. It was important for the changes that probably don't show to others, but you and I know about. I wouldn't have changed as much without the insight, but I could still have made a lot of changes even without it."

Marjorie had put first how she was treated—that is, the therapy could not have taken place without the establishment of a certain quality of relationship between us. Since I always respected her, even at her sickest, and since she was able to perceive this, then that relationship was established and grew. She put understanding or insight second without which the degree of growth or change would have been a great deal less.

Most of us do not know why we have become the way we are. Marjorie knew, by the time she entered treatment as a woman in her midthirties, that she disliked her mother, who had been a poor mother. She did not realize that her mother had been crazy for years, and that the sadistic persecution of her daughter was a chief symptom of that psychosis. She did not understand that she could not have elicited her mother's torturing and vilification of her had her mother been normal. As it was, the daughter's even better than average behavior as a child was always misinterpreted and maligned because of the mother's starkly pathological personality, something over which the child could have no control.

Marjorie's torturers, who began to attack her so early in her life, induced a great sense of unworthiness and guilt in her. As would any child, she felt that something must be terribly bad about her to bring about such treatment by others. She felt guilty that her lack of worth as a person caused her to disturb those around her. Coming to know and understand these things was of great importance. She was able to change from someone who always blamed herself to a person who saw clearly the role that others, as well as she, played in these terrors. Understanding allows one not to be as afraid, nor as uncertain, and to feel less guilty. It is not, of course, only the understanding of others which is important: of cardinal significance is the understanding of oneself. One cannot use oneself well, or treat oneself sensibly, if one does not know who one is and what one needs. A realistic appreciation of one's own drives, capacities, skills, potentials, frustrations, and longings is the key to achieving satisfaction.

Alvin came to treatment in the midst of a deep, despairing depression. It had been precipitated by the leaving of his friend, with whom he had lived and worked for almost ten years, and with whom he had had a variable homosexual relationship. One day his friend simply announced that he was leaving and walked out. Alvin was stunned. As the months passed, he became more and more dazed and confused, and fell deep into a depressive morass.

Alvin had considered for some years that he might seek psychoanalysis, since in many ways his life felt unsatisfactory to him. He was successful at his work, and had many superficial friends, but felt deeply unhappy. He had taken himself to be basically homosexual. He had never had intercourse with a woman, although his social relations with them were positive. His friend had highly negative attitudes toward women, spoke of them condescendingly, and assumed that both he and Alvin were much better off for never trusting a woman.

All of this came under scrutiny in Alvin's treatment. His first understanding involved his feelings about his former friend. He had somehow kept himself from perceiving all that was negative, even destructive in that relationship.

"I thought of Charles as the best friend I had ever had," he said.

"Perhaps he was."

"Perhaps. But that means that I have never had a friend I could really trust. I wanted to believe that he had my welfare at heart, but now I see how wrong I was. I did so much for him. It is terribly hard to accept the extent to which he used me."

"It is clear how opportunistic he was being. He stayed as long as it was profitable and convenient," I said.

"That's right. He took off at the first opportunity to do better."

"How does that make you feel?"

"Terrible. No wonder I was so depressed. It isn't only that he left. I see now that he left with no regrets, no sense of loss, and no concern for me."

Alvin also began to see how large a part he had played in all this. His early life, with a powerful and demanding mother and a quiet and accommodating father, had made him acquiescent to a fault. Losses early in his life had sensitized him to so fear loss that he would go to any lengths to avoid being left by someone close to him. That way he left himself always open to being used, even emotionally blackmailed. He maintained a consistently cheerful demeanor which denied the pain he was feeling underneath. As he became aware of his anger and his passive acquiescence, his depression cleared, and he began to attempt to have more control of his own life.

"You have known for some time now how Charles took advantage of you."

"Yes, but now I have begun to feel the anger. The bastard—how could he do that to me? What a nerve! I'm through protecting him in my own mind from the realization of what he is really like. What a fool I was to let him treat me that way!"

Alvin realized that his homosexual preference was less by internal imperative and more by fear of the alternative. He began to date women, with great initial caution. As the months and years passed he found that indeed his preference, both social and sexual, was for a heterosexual mode of life. His first satisfactory experience with intercourse was of enormous significance to him, and was a watershed experience which marked a turning in his intimate relations with others.

"Guess what?" Alvin asked me.

"What?"

"I finally made it. I had intercourse last night."

"How was it?"

"Not great, but not bad. Nothing like what I feared."

"How was it different?"

"She was very considerate of me. As I told you two days ago, she doesn't seem to be very experienced either. But she wanted it to work out for both of us."

"Rather different from Charles's view of women."

"And from mine. It's stupid, but I feel as though I've achieved some enormous success."

"You have."

"Oh no, to anyone else it would be nothing."

"It means a great deal. You've got past a fear you have had for so many years."

"That's right. I feel great—really encouraged to go on trying to change things for myself. Mind you, we were like two inexperienced kids. But I'm proud of myself."

"Good."

Alvin's life was, as is every life, a most complex tapestry, woven out of his past experiences and including his present relationships. Many hours over several years were spent following the themes and the events of his life, understanding what others had done, and what he had done and why. It was that understanding which first relieved him of the symptom of depression and then allowed him to begin to make very different choices. Those choices began to address his needs, which he no longer was able to deny. They also made him *selective in the people he became close to, so that both he and they derived much greater benefit from their friendships.*

In this case Alvin was able to change from a homosexual to a heterosexual life-style. This is a result which occurs only in a small minority of homosexuals. Most do not wish to change their sexual orientation, and most recognize that, even should they try, they would be unable to do so. The most frequent way in which homosexuals are helped by psychotherapy is that they come to live more comfortably with themselves and with others, accepting their sexual orientation and avoiding those conflicts which led to the depression and anxiety which brought them to the therapist. However, in some instances, and Alvin was an example, treatment allows a shift to occur to another mode of sexual adjustment.

It is easy when talking about insight to create an unjusti-fied mystique about what it is that needs to be known through psychotherapy. There is no special area of knowl-edge which is known only to psychotherapists, and is at the heart of everyone's problems. All kinds of difficulties and painful facts and feelings are the cause of people's troubles. There are many who fall into the trap of thinking they have discovered what it is that causes neuroses. There is no pat-tern, no one single complex, or specific deficiency which exists to explain what lies behind most personal difficulties. All manner of secrets lie hidden from the outside world, and even from one's inside awareness. So the answer to the ques-tion: "What is it that one tries to understand in psychother-apy?" is simply: "Everything."

Seeing, knowing, and expressing the truth are the greatest freedoms. Virtually no one is in the position of being able to do so completely. The most fortunate person is the one who comes as close to this as possible. Freud was correct in his understanding that one had to get to the truth to be well and free. He mistook *what* truth was hidden, as have so many others before and since. It is not *one* truth. There is no single cardinal problem which accounts for the troubles of mankind: not aggression, not sexual inhibition, not trauma during birth, not narcissistic self-love, not incestuous conflict, not errors in one phase of the process of separation and individuation, not any one area of content over all others. Stress and strain arise from a myriad of sources. Successful psychotherapy seeks to reveal and understand all those sources. Much of the truth is simple, although it has a profound effect upon the person involved. It may be as simple a matter as a patient's deep recognition that no one cares for her, despite all protestations and pretence of the opposite.

Some truths are important in the lives of all of us. For example, a major dilemma in life is the following one: On the one hand, we need to be attached to people all our lives, otherwise we feel lost and incomplete and starved; on the other hand, we need to have a sense of separateness and autonomy about ourselves, so that we are not always locked in with those people and we can be ourselves. There is no human being who doesn't struggle with these two opposing needs. However, that conflict is not the cause of neurosis, or schizophrenia, or character disorder, or any other problem. It is simply one of the stresses or pressures which contributes to such disorders in people. The insight we seek is the recognition of the multitude of stresses which play upon the patient. Paul Horton calls the comfort that all of us seek from other people, from activities, or from objects that take the place of other people, *solace*.

The interventions on the part of the therapist that are needed are those which allow the true inner and outer reality of the patient to be seen, perceived, and it is hoped, accepted.

For it is that which is denied or invisible which is uncomfortable and even dangerous. Understanding helps in many ways. It decreases the likelihood that one will feel unable to accept oneself. It makes it more likely that one will make informed choices which will, in turn, lead to greater satisfaction. It makes one less a victim of the unknown, since less is unknown. It makes one aware of one's patterns of behavior, and where they came from, so that one is in a better position to change them. It diminishes the difference between how one presents to the world and how one feels about oneself on the inside. This in turn gives a person a greater feeling of always being the same, in different external circumstances, as well as on the inside. This makes him feel and appear to others more valid, more real, more authentic; that is, as having a greater degree of inner and outer consistency and integrity. Having the patient reach this understanding is one of my chief goals in therapy.

Understanding is occasionally achieved suddenly, but usually it is not. In intensive psychotherapy, sometimes there is a new and sudden realization which did not exist before. Then the patient will say: "That really helps. It is something I didn't see, but now it is quite clear."

"I've always been that way," said Clara. "It is no different with you than it was with my parents and the men in my life. When someone hurts me by leaving, I turn 360 degrees and think: 'Now they are gone. I will look elsewhere and find someone else'."

"I think that you made a slip," I suggested.

"What was that?"

"Although you are not very good at mathematics, I think you know what a 360-degree turn is."

"Oh, you are right. That means I have . . ." She paused.

"You have turned all the way around so that you are still facing the person—looking for the person."

"I did say that. I guess I do mean that. I pretend I don't care, but I still do. I am hurt and am too proud to show it. That is very clear. That is what I always do."

Such sudden realizations happen only occasionally: usually understanding comes in small steps, by going over the same thing repeatedly and trying out various options until one finds those which seem to fit best.

An unnecessary and inexact distinction is often made in regard to the different ways in which the therapist intervenes in order to achieve understanding. Psychoanalysts sometimes say that the word *interpretation* should be reserved for when the analyst is revealing something that is truly unconscious, and that those more superficial interventions about conscious material might be called *clarifications*. This distinction is misleading, since all explanations are likely to operate at both conscious and unconscious levels. To speak of pure "interpretation" pretends to a kind of exactness that does not and cannot exist in treatment.

How does understanding come about? Not by long silences on the part of the therapist, very occasionally broken by terse, exact, and all-revealing interpretations. A therapist who believes that he should know the answer and give it to the patient is misguided. For knowing cannot be achieved without the help and cooperation of the patient. The truth is best arrived at by give and take between the two participants. The initial role of the patient is to provide as much information and background as he can. The role of the therapist is to hear and remember ideas and tentative understandings. The ideas go back and forth, the therapist suggesting possible explanations from time to time, the patient "trying them on for size." The therapist, because of his training, is able to make appropriate educated guesses. The patient, because it is his history and his life, is in a position to explore what has happened to him and how he has felt. The therapist, because it is another person whose life is being examined, can be more objective, for his feelings are not at risk as much as if it were his own life. The patient, once he realizes that he is the therapist's source of information, in fact his guide, has a growing confidence in his right and his ability to dissect and understand the matters at hand, namely, his own life.

This dialogue between the two people allows them to approach and even arrive at the truth. Reality is always being assessed. The patient, in the midst of his life and his feelings, may see things in a distorted way, in order to protect his vulnerabilities, or because he has developed, over the years, a host of defensive blind spots and prejudices. The therapist, not as immersed in the material that so deeply affects the patient, can change the way in which the patient sees and interprets things. This occurs not in large leaps, but rather in very small steps which go back and forth and back and forth along the road to understanding.

The process is one of refinement, and is very much like tuning an instrument, such as a short-wave radio, or a microscope. At first one is happy just to have got the signal into range, or the field in view. Later, in order to hear or see quite clearly, much finer tuning must take place.

Barbara had been in therapy once a week for several years. In the eyes of the world, and of her professional colleagues in her work in the arts, she was remarkably successful. Inside, it had not felt that way to her. She had always been lonely. She had always felt very different from those around her: not that she was in the right, but rather that she had always been in the wrong. For example, her husband had taken great advantage of her over many years, but she had felt that somehow she had been failing in her obligations to him.

More recently this was less the case. She had not become more blaming of others, nor had she lost any of her surprising humility, but she had come to see that often, even usually, what she felt was justified, fair, and realistic. This was one of her most important insights.

"It is hard to believe," she said one day.

"What is?" I asked. Barbara reflected for a moment. "That I could have lived as long as I did without seeing or knowing what I was doing. I must be very stupid."

I laughed. "I'm afraid not," I ventured. "Your work indicates that there must be another explanation."

"The amazing fact is that one can manage not to see what is going on. Now I see more and more what is happening. I guess the hardest part was to allow myself to begin to see my real self and to appreciate what other people are really like. It still embarrasses me that I could have been so blind."

"It is surprising, when you think of it," I agreed. "You are someone who has always been highly intuitive about people. Your choices of those whom you hire to work with you shows that. And yet you were able to be unaware of so much of what was going on around you and inside of you."

"It must be stupidity. What else could explain it?"

"Pain explains it. Pain which you felt, and pain which you tried to avoid feeling."

"What pain do you mean?" she asked.

"The pain of seeing that your mother cared for you in a very limited way—that your success pleased her because of what it brought to her, and not because of her pleasure in what it brought to you. The pain of realizing that you were born much more gifted than your brother, and that, although you had no wish to hurt him, your successes have contributed to his chronic sense of defeat. The pain of knowing that despite all the people about you, you were always lonely, and there was virtually no one with whom you really felt close. The pain of facing up to the fact that you have always considered yourself basically deficient, and deserving of unhappiness and loneliness. And the pain of recognizing that so many of your most intensely personal drives—physical and emotional—had not been and were unlikely to be gratified." She was silent for a while. "What are you thinking?" I asked.

"I think what you say is right. It is the pain that matters: and, even more important, the avoidance of pain." She shook her head slowly. "It is hard to believe, isn't it?"

6

A LIVING MACHINE
Mind in Body

KATHLEEN was sixty years of age and in excellent physical health. Her four children were successful and accomplished, and she was proud of them and of her four grandchildren. One day her daughter, whom I had known since childhood, called me.

"Mother seems changed, but it is hard to put your finger on it."

"What have you noticed?"

"You remember how she always had a great memory for people and events? Well, that has slipped. Also, sometimes she just stares blankly while all of us are talking. The other day she got confused while out shopping and for a while couldn't find her way back to the house. I wonder if she is depressed."

I had her daughter bring Kathleen in to see me. In almost every way she was normal, physically and emotionally. But on clinical questions to test her mental functioning there was evidence of some loss of intellectual capacity, most particularly in recent memory. I referred her to a neurologist who said that her memory capacity was still in the normal range, but that the history of change was most important. He performed a brain scan which demonstrated that widespread loss of brain cells, still moderate in degree, had begun to take place. This was the early stage of progressive dementia.

No active treatment for the basic illness was available. The dementia progressed so that over the next seven years Kathleen became more and more disabled and dependent upon others. After three years she was in a nursing home. In time she could recognize none of the people around her. She was given good medical and nursing care until she died. Making the medical diagnosis was important for two principal reasons: the patient was given the general care she required, and did not miss any active treatment she might have required, for example, should she have turned out to be depressed.

Disappointing and sad as it was, the family came to know what the situation was and what it would probably be in the future, and were able to make the best arrangements possible. In the painful years that followed, the role of the therapist was not in helping the patient directly, but in helping her through supporting and advising her family in the difficult choices which they had to make on her behalf.

In matters of the mind, the body cannot be ignored. The brain is the home of both the intellect and the emotions, so that any physical or chemical problem within the central nervous system may present as a change in the mental or emotional state of the person. When patients are treated in psychotherapy someone must determine that no physical illness is present. When the psychotherapist is a psychiatrist, he can assume responsibility for both the patient's psychological and physical state of health.

Because his basic training has been in medicine, he will be aware of the possible links between the mind and the body. People often ask a psychiatrist: "What is the use of all those years of medical school and internship? Couldn't you learn to practice psychiatry with only a very limited knowledge of medicine?" When I am asked such questions, I reply: "As in all of medicine, it is not sufficient to learn treatment techniques only. One must recognize the problem which the treatment is intended to help with or to cure. To be able to make an informed diagnosis requires full medical training."

A psychiatrist who spends much of his time practicing psychotherapy may rarely if ever use his stethoscope to listen to a heart; but most medical and surgical diagnoses are made, at least provisionally, by carefully listening to the patient's history. And so the psychiatrist, taking a careful medical history as part of his psychiatric evaluation, might find clues to possible medical pathology which will require treament. For example, cancer of the pancreas very often shows itself through a severe depression. Tumors of the brain can cause almost any behavioral disorder. Epilepsy, especially arising from the lobes at the side of the brain (the temporal lobes), can cause severe emotional outbursts. Systemic diseases such as high blood pressure, diabetes, or multiple sclerosis can cause fleeting and confusing symptoms, which must not be taken to be the result of conflicting emotions. In some cases the psychiatrist may conduct medical tests himself in order to confirm or deny his suspicion that the patient has a medical problem. Or he may refer the patient to a colleague of another medical specialty to arrange for further tests to complete the diagnostic assessment. In either case it is only when the possibility of organic disease has been ruled out that he is free to proceed with whatever form of therapy is most appropriate for the person in question.

When the psychotherapist is not a physician the same principle must be applied. In this case the patient can be examined by his family physician who will be the general medical consultant and conduct whatever investigations and treatments are required. He can also refer the patient to any specialists should that be necessary. As the patient goes on in psychotherapy the therapist and the family physician then have a partnership where it is understood that each has in mind the area of responsibility of the other. In that way the patient is assured that his needs as a whole person will be met.

In the relationship between mind and body it is possible that the patient presenting emotional or mental disturbances may have some medical problem. This problem may either be causing symptoms which are physical, such as pain or dizziness, or emotional, such as anxiety or depression. A physician must be able to diagnose the cause of the problem before he can decide what the nature of the treatment should be.

I had known Morris and his wife over many years. One day his wife called me. "He has not been himself for a year or so. It has come on gradually. He doesn't sleep well, is restless and unhappy. He seems to be becoming more and more depressed. He has been unwilling to see a psychiatrist, because he says there's nothing that anyone can do—he feels quite hopeless. Finally he has agreed to come and see you."

We met in my office a few days later. Morris was fifty-six years of age and had, as any person that age has, numerous factors which could have contributed toward his being depressed. But there were other symptoms as well which caused me concern. He had headaches which had gradually worsened in recent months. He was sometimes suddenly forgetful and even disoriented. I referred him to a neurologist for full examination of his central nervous system, including specialized tests.

The tests revealed that Morris had a tumor of the frontal lobe of his brain. He was operated on the following week and subsequently had a reasonably comfortable eight months. In time the symptoms returned. He had a second operation to relieve him temporarily, but the tumor had been malignant, and he was dead almost exactly a year after his visit to my office.

The principal symptom was depression, but to a medical person the history suggested organic brain disease. In this instance making the diagnosis did not save the patient, for it happened that the pathological lesion was, unfortunately, not open to curative treatment. All that could be given to Morris was a few more months of relatively comfortable life.

In other instances the underlying medical problem may be treatable, and it is essential not to embark upon psychotherapeutic treatment when valid medical or surgical treatment will be curative. I have mentioned Marjorie (in chapter 5) as someone who has benefited a great deal from the insight gained from years of psychotherapy. One part of her treatment was quite different and, I believe, instructive.

When we had been working together for several years, Marjorie was faced with a medical emergency. She had a silent gastric ulcer which, while I was away on holiday, bled, suddenly and severely. She was rushed to hospital in shock, given blood, and most of her stomach was removed in an emergency operation. By the time I returned, the surgery had taken place and she was recuperating.

Some months later, Marjorie was still not feeling physically well, though she had recovered from the surgical intervention. She now had chronic diarrhea, caused by the changes in her gastrointestinal tract which the surgery had made. She was able to cope with the diarrhea, but as more months passed she had other more intangible symptoms. She felt weak and tired, which was atypical of her. She slept badly, had no energy while awake, often experienced palpitations of her heart upon exertion. Her mood was more variable than it had ever been; she seemed more unstable and easier to upset. Her family physician, knowing she had been a patient in psychotherapy for some years, took these symptoms to be a further elaboration of her neurotic difficulties. She got worse and worse. Finally I referred her to a gastroenterologist, because I felt that some physical problem lay behind her difficulties. He concluded that the diarrhea was due to her inability to absorb certain foods; because of the operation she had developed an intolerance of fatty foods. As a result, through the chronic diarrhea, she had developed several severe and progressive vitamin deficiencies. He altered her diet and prescribed vitamins by injection. All of these new symptoms disappeared and as she has maintained the same dietary regimen, they have not returned.

We went on with psychotherapy, which continued to be useful. In this case a valid medical illness might easily have been taken to be of psychological origin, and proper treatment would have been missed. Such an error would have led to a continuing deterioration of her health.

Just as physical or organic causes can produce symptoms which appear to be of emotional origin, the converse may be true: that is, symptoms which are physical in nature may have emotional roots. An important example of this is hypochondriasis, where the patient feels certain that he has a serious illness, and has chronic aches and pains and a variety of physical discomforts. Here too, the physician will arrange for careful physical examination, probably including any special tests for various physical illnesses.

In this case, once physical causes have been ruled out, it is not sufficient to say that the problem is "emotional in origin," or that it is "all in the patient's head." Both these conclusions do nothing to correct the problem. Once this opinion has been reached, the patient should be referred to a psychiatrist, to see if he has some treatment to offer. If, for example, the hypochondriasis arises out of chronic depression in the patient, then that depression requires and deserves treatment, in the same way as does any medical condition. The first treatment of the depression might be symptomatic, such as prescribing antidepressant medication, which may directly attack the state of depression. The second treatment of the depression might aim at finding and addressing its roots, that is, by engaging the patient in psychotherapy.

Donald was referred for psychiatric treatment after years of medical care which had led to no improvement in his severe symptoms. He lived in a small town, and over a period of ten years he had tried in vain to get help for dizziness, chest and neck pain, attacks of fearfulness, and severe bouts of exhaustion in which he felt he was about to die.

Donald had been treated repeatedly by all of the several doctors in his town. He had also been referred to consultants in a larger city which was a university center. Many different diagnoses were offered, implicating his heart, his lungs, and his endocrine glands. He had been given a variety of medications, most of which impaired him, and upon some of which (tranquillizers) he had become dependent. He had been admitted to the hospital numerous times. Finally his doctors, after years of seeking tangible physical causes of his complaints, decided by a process of elimination that they were probably of emotional origin. He was referred for psychiatric treatment. It required two years of treatment before Donald was able to be free of all medication.

"I feel terrible," Donald said one day, "and I can't help blaming you and the doctors who preceded you."

"How is it our fault?"

"It is theirs for putting me on those damn pills. It is yours for taking me off them. I know that is unreasonable, but that is how I feel."

"That is how you feel, but what are you doing about it?"

"I know you are right in insisting that I have to get free of the stuff before I can really improve. So what I am doing is what both of us know I have to do. I have gradually reduced the dose until this week, for the first time I have taken nothing. It is a terrific temptation to take something when I feel pain or anxiety, but so far I have resisted the temptation."

"You have done the hardest part already. It will not be easy for a long time, but it will keep becoming somewhat easier."

"I know. No more easy ways out. I have to keep facing up to all those feelings about my wife and my parents that I have avoided for so long. That is in some ways the worst pain."

As Donald had said, the psychotherapy revealed that he was full of anxiety and tension that resulted from family conflicts, and that gave rise to his physical symptoms of dizziness, pain, and enervation. He and I worked on these for several years, with the result that he became free of these attacks, and free of all physical symptoms. He went from being someone who was constantly afraid of having a life-threatening illness and was always consulting physicians, to someone who lived an active and comfortable life, free of the necessity of consulting with doctors.

It would not have been possible to conclude quickly that Donald's problems were not of physical origin. Since the symptoms were so much like those that can arise from, for example, heart disease or thyroid gland disease, it was essential to take the greatest care to eliminate the possibility of the existence of such disorders. However, that process continued too long. This was partly due to a lack of confidence in psychiatric treatment on the part of some of Donald's physicians. They may have had disappointing results with patients whom they had referred for psychiatric treatment. Or, being in a small town where no psychiatrist was available, they might not have been fully aware of the help that psychiatric care in the hands of a proficient practitioner could offer. But the main reason was their hesitation to suggest to him that he was in need of psychiatric treatment, for they had come to expect that patients would take offence at such an opinion, believing that it meant that they were considered very abnormal. In the end there was no alternative, Donald was referred to a psychiatrist and was able, finally, to get to the true source of his problems.

There is another relationship between mind and body

which the psychotherapist must bear in mind. The body has evolved to be used. It is a living machine which flourishes under certain optimal conditions: normal weight, normal nutrition, and a sufficient amount of activity and exercise. A grossly obese middle-aged man treated with psychotherapy will not end up free of symptoms if his obesity continues. The body of a patient who eats poorly and who is sedentary will object in some fashion. These symptoms might include chronic lethargy, lack of enthusiasm, aches of joints or muscles, hypersensitivity to temperature change, or chronic low mood. The psychotherapist must be aware of the fact that the abused or neglected body will somehow cry out for better treatment by its owner. In raising with the patient the lack of respect he shows his body, the therapist may ultimately make him aware of the need to change his style of living.

Some therapists believe that all of this has nothing to do with psychotherapy, and hence is not the concern of the psychotherapist; such an attitude is most unrealistic. Good health requires not only the treatment of existing symptoms but the prevention of future and avoidable symptoms. The obese patient may give clear evidence of conflicts about his parents and his siblings. Becoming aware of those conflicts may make him more able to do what he has to do: namely, modify his food intake and his activity pattern so that in time his weight becomes normal. For the obesity dictates that he will have numerous symptoms both physical and psychological which cannot be got rid of as long as the problem of abnormal weight exists.

Harold is an extremely intelligent engineer who has made a considerable success of his career in industry. At the age of fifty-two he had fulfilled the promise of his early brilliance in school and was content with his life in general. He came to therapy because of difficulties with his adolescent children, which were gradually, and successfully resolved. In the course of the treatment his style of life was discussed, for over a period of five years he had had a series of medical and surgical problems—prostatic disease as well as kidney and gallbladder stones were included. He led an inactive life physically and through gaining five to ten pounds a year had become considerably obese. It was concluded in the therapy that Harold suffered in numerous ways from the neglect of his body.

He changed markedly his style of eating to a diet low in fat and protein and high in naturally occurring carbohydrates. He increased his activity through walking and swimming regularly. Over half a year he gradually lost most of his excess weight.

"I feel so much better now. The things I worked out in therapy were very helpful with my boys, and with Myrna, and even with my work. What has come from my change in life-style is at least as important to my general sense of well-being."

"How does it help you?"

'First of all, I feel more alert and alive all the time." He laughed. "At work they always told me I drove them nuts because I think and talk too fast. Now I think and talk even faster. I don't have the aches and pains I took for granted as being part of getting older. And my prostatic problem has improved—I have a much stronger urinary stream."

"Those are all very important. Anything else?"

"Yes, After I swim I have a sense of well-being that I don't achieve in any other way. I now believe that a lot of the low moods which I and other people experience are a result of inactivity. That prolonged lift I get after half an hour in the pool is like a shot in the arm."

"It is a shot, internally, of your own body chemicals which raise your mood—a safe shot without the side-effects of foreign chemicals."

"Right. Also, I am able to wear those great Harris Tweed jackets I had bought in England when I was in the service, and which hung in my closet all those years. I'm proud of how well I look, enjoy the *compliments I get from other people, and am pleased that I have had the persistence to achieve my goal."*

"You have a right to be proud and pleased. You have achieved a lot, all of which ensures a better and longer life for you."

"Thanks. It feels very good to me."

Harold saw and said it clearly. What he had achieved in psychotherapy was of great importance. The portion of his success which had come from the better care of his body could not have come about in any other way. So the well-being of the mind depends a great deal upon the well-being of the body, and the psychotherapist must of necessity have an interest in both.

All psychotherapists must be aware that the home of the mind, that is the person, is the brain. Without normal function of the brain there cannot be normal function of the mind. I have given an example of brain disease, a tumor, which demanded recognition before rational treatment could be instituted. There are other forms of brain disease which affect a much larger proportion of the population than do brain tumors, namely wasting of the brain cells themselves. As the number of older people in the population increases, the number of cases of organic brain disorder of this kind also increases. This disturbance, as we saw with Kathleen, includes memory loss, intellectual impairment, progressing even to disorientation, and finally incompetence in some elderly people. It also includes that same collection of symptoms arising in younger patients, perhaps in their fifties or even forties, a situation which used to be called presenile dementia. We now recognize that, whatever the age of onset of this disease, the pathology involved is a similar death of brain cells, with the inevitable accompaniment of loss of function. Such loss is permanent, because once a brain cell dies it can never recover, nor will it be replaced by another similar cell.

There is another connection between mind and body which is of the greatest importance. It is not only the physical integrity of brain cells which influences the state of the mind and of the emotions. It is also the chemical environment of the brain which has a fundamental influence. For this reason, psychological treatment, that is psychotherapy, is not the only or even best treatment for all emotional disturbances. Severe depression ordinarily responds best to antidepressant medications and, in those few instances in which it does not, to electroshock. Manic-depressive illness is usually markedly improved with Lithium. These are only two examples of essential treatments the use of which must not be neglected in appropriate cases. After the medication has begun to do its work, then it can be determined to what further extent psychotherapy may be of value.

It is not the case that medications are indicated in most instances of emotional disturbance. The large majority of patients will be successfully treated with psychotherapy alone. But a very significant minority will deserve and even require chemical treatments, the neglect of which will constitute inadequate and even improper care.

The mind cannot be treated in a vacuum: it exists within the body and depends upon the body for its integrity. And so psychotherapeutic treatment cannot be divorced from consideration of the health of the body, that is, structural, chemical, and electrical health. Only when it has been adequately attended to can the therapist then turn his attention to the therapy of the mind.

7

GIVE AND TAKE, EBB AND FLOW
Dependence and Interdependence

THE interdependence which develops during the course of psychotherapy serves one principal purpose, namely the growth of the patient, and his ultimate autonomy. The period of dependence which must necessarily precede the achievement of this goal should only last long enough for the patient's needs to be filled. He should then be allowed to become free, to make his own choices as to how and when he can take appropriate steps to further his own development.

James is a psychoanalyst in late middle life. As a young psychiatrist, he decided that he would like to go more deeply into his work with his patients, so he undertook psychoanalytic training which included a personal analysis.

One curious and disturbing result of his treatment was that he seemed to have given up a part of himself to his analyst, a part that was never recovered. Even when he had become a senior analyst in his own right, this connection remained very evident. In discussions within the psychoanalytic society he was to be found taking the same side of an argument as his former analyst. At social functions they would be together, pleased and stimulated by each other's company, or probably more correctly, by their mutual agreement and admiration. James appeared to have found something he had long been seeking and, in finding it, been diminished in the process.

One is left to speculate about what had occurred in the analysis. It appears that an unspoken agreement was made by both parties in the treatment. James would always look up to and admire his analyst, who would in turn give James the feeling of importance which derives from being the accepted disciple of a great person.

This illustration is given to indicate how easy it is for something to go awry in the process of individuation. From the patient's point of view it is very tempting to accept the invitation to surrender a portion of his autonomy. This way one is always assured of affection or love. Such devotion is dearly bought.

During the months and years of intensive psychotherapy, the treatment and the therapist may come to predominate in the mind of the patient, taking precedence over all other considerations: his work, his friends, even his family. It is essential, when this is the case, that both parties keep the real situation in perspective. The treatment may at that moment be the single most important activity in the patient's life. But it is *not* his life. His life is outside the consulting room, where ultimately he must be able to satisfy his needs. In time the therapy will have to fade in significance and the therapist will play less of a part in the patient's thoughts and feelings.

Laura spent four years with me in psychoanalysis. She was feeling in need of analysis because of her painful sensitivity. She was quiet with others, painfully so, and flushed easily when embarrassed. She was very hesitant, even apologetic, when she approached me: I agreed to accept her for treatment.

In the early months of the analysis she was diffident and excessively self-blaming. She had been reared by crude, insensitive par-

ents who put no value upon her sensitivity. Her artistic gifts had no interest for them—they wished her to find some ordinary work, become self-supporting and supporting of them as soon as possible. She was unduly grateful for the opportunity which the analysis afforded because her lack of confidence made her certain that an analyst would have many more important and interesting people to analyze. Her natural tendency was to give over to me. What I thought and said were considered by her to be infinitely more important than anything she might think or say.

Gradually, as she grew aware of the painful feelings, thoughts, and fears which were such a burden to her, Laura became more able to speak her mind in the analysis. She continued to find it difficult or impossible to express any negative concerns about me because she felt enormously dependent on my goodwill. During the second half of the analysis, she became less shy and more self-assertive. She questioned me, cautiously but firmly, then differed from me when she found some explanation of mine inadequate. She challenged her husband on the limitations which their marriage put upon her, which she knew she had cooperated with him in instituting, and they became more equal partners.

In the analysis she became more able to find explanations of her own. Finally, she was able to see me as a capable person who wanted to help, but one who fell far short of her original idealized image of him. Where earlier I had occupied most of her fantasies and dreams and she had seen me as infallible, knowing all the answers to her problems, she now saw me as someone who had played an important yet limited role in her growth and development.

When the time came to consider stopping the analysis, Laura spoke with appreciation about what had transpired. She now thought of me as a good friend—someone who had been available at the right time to assist her in doing something that she had, within herself, become ready to do. She had lost all of her apologetic stance by now, and was less passive in her life, having undertaken more serious steps in her career as an artist. I helped her to recognize both her sadness and her pleasure at leaving me. She was sorry to give up *our regular, frequent meetings. She was gratified to use her own capacity to take control of her life. Her final hour was both sad and happy. She was sorry to leave her analyst–friend, but glad to move on.*

In the years since she stopped the analysis, Laura and I have met briefly on four or five occasions. We talk for a few moments, I enquire about recent events, she asks about my life and my welfare. Both of us remember the closeness and intimacy of that former period of our relationship, the period which I call the "active phase" of the treatment. When we meet, it is clear that a great change has occurred: we do not discuss our relationship, for this is no longer appropriate. We are two people who have successfully completed a difficult task and have gone our separate ways.

In each of us a part remains which attaches to the other. But that is now a very modest bond, although still reflecting that more intense connection that existed years before.

In the case of Laura, she came to analysis as a very vulnerable patient, ready to make a change in her life which she could not make alone. Not only was it clear to both of us how much she relied on me, but she was able to let this show. With many patients this is not the case. Their instinctive fear of allowing anyone to take advantage of them makes them deny that the therapist is of vital importance to them. In such instances much work must be done to change this attitude, so that in time the patient can accept his dependence on the therapist, recognizing that it is only a temporary situation that will lead to his maturation.

That the relationship is mutual need be no secret within the therapeutic relationship. The practice of psychotherapy is creative and rewarding for the therapist. He derives many satisfactions from the patient who is a partner in his work. When a patient is seriously ill, it will not occur to him that he could give anything of value to the therapist. He may very well imagine that the therapist is not only an ideal person, but has an ideal life, and needs nothing, particularly from the worthless person the patient feels himself to be.

Of course there are some patients who are highly suspicious of the therapist, and alert to the possibility that he might try to rob them of their already diminished personal supplies.

Helen was in a rage. I wanted to change the time of her appointment.

"How dare you treat me the way you do?"

"How do I treat you?"

"You take me for granted: you expect to have everything your own way. You have a full life, mine is empty. I cannot stand the fact that I have to come here and I have to tell you about myself. Now you want me to change my time. Why should your wishes or needs come before mine?"

"I try to pay attention to your needs whenever I can."

"It isn't enough. It infuriates me that you can be so unconcerned about me. Everything always has to be your way, but that's the story of my life, dammit. I suppose I have to agree to change the hour, but I wish I could be unreasonable and refuse to give in."

"Thank you. I hope we won't have to make any more changes for a while."

Helen felt that her life was preposterous. She was stung by what she perceived as my selfishness and was unwilling to accept what she saw as an injustice.

Throughout life people depend on one another. In any successful relationship, including a therapeutic one, it is essential that there is give and take between the two people involved. When psychotherapy begins, the patient's needs are so great that the therapist must do most of the giving. At that stage the therapist recognizes that it has to be that way, and does not resent the imbalance. As the treatment progresses and the patient becomes stronger, he will be able to give more and take less and the relationship will become more balanced. The patient will feel more equal to the therapist than when they first started working together, and will be able to tell him so. He will see that the therapist also has needs and even limitations, and that not only does he learn from the therapist, but the therapist learns from him. Various patients handle this growing awareness in different ways.

Brenda came for treatment when she was fifteen years of age. She seemed to be bright but she could not succeed at school. She would get into an obsessional tangle about her work, trying to make it so perfect that she could not complete it.

She was referred to me through a member of her family who knew me personally. For the first four months she had to be in a hospital because she was overwhelmed with anxiety, depression, and an enormous sense of apprehension. This was followed by intensive psychotherapy, four times a week to start with, and later less frequently.

Therapy was painful and frightening. Brenda feared that I would be as intrusive as her family had always been. She worried that I would be their agent and protect their interests, not hers. She expected that she would discover that she was not only incompetent but deeply disturbed. As the months and years passed she was able to learn to trust me, and to expose her multitude of fears and feelings of shame. Along with this, she gradually grew calmer and more sure of herself, in time returned to work, and ultimately made a very good adjustment to life.

In about the fifth year of her treatment I was taken ill. The interruption of treatment at that time was not crucial for Brenda, as it would have been a few years earlier. Still, she felt uncomfortable, and was uncertain of how to deal with the fact that I, who had become very important to her, was ill at home in bed. I, in turn, was trying to cope with being off work and unable to see patients for the very first time. I was experiencing the feeling that I was letting down my patients who were in need of help. I was missing all those gratifications that come to the therapist through working with his patients.

One day Brenda was with her relative who had referred her to me. "How do you feel about his being ill?" he asked.

"I feel very bad about it," she replied. "I can get along all right without him for a while, but I am sorry he is ill."

"What have you done about it?"

She was embarrassed. "Nothing. I have thought about it, but I don't know if it is right to do anything."

"Of course it is," he replied. "He would be glad to hear from you."

"Do you really think so?" Brenda asked.

"I am sure of it," he asked.

The next day a package was delivered to my home. It contained a goldfish in a bowl, and a tin of fish food. A note was attached, which read: "This is Sam. He may not be clever, but he will be a good friend. I hope you enjoy his company."

I was touched by the warmth and concern evidenced by this gesture. The patient took advantage of a natural opportunity to show me how she valued what I had done for her and how much she cared about my welfare. These were feelings she would otherwise have been too shy to express.

The patient–therapist relationship, in terms of interdependency, runs a similar course to the child–parent relationship. There is one important difference: in most cases the parent and child will maintain some contact as long as they are both alive, whereas in the therapeutic relationship this does not usually occur. There are some exceptions: for example, a patient may be so damaged that he continues to see the therapist for many years or even decades. A candidate in training to become a psychoanalyst may eventually become a colleague of his former analyst. On a few occasions the therapist and patient may remain friends when the treatment has ended.

Between a parent and his child the early years of the relationship involve a flow much more predominantly from the one who is in a stronger position (the parent) to the one who is in the more needful position (the child). But should both live long enough, the time will eventually come when the main flow is in the opposite direction. The middle-aged parent discovers many ways in which his son or daughter is better equipped than himself. As the years pass, this interdependency shifts more and more in that same direction until, in the case of the elderly parent, it may ultimately come about that the child now entirely gives to or looks after his parent.

A similar change in a relationship may occur between former patient and aging therapist if they have maintained contact. As the years pass the latter may become considerably more needful and expect more from his former patient than has ever been the case before. This shift in dependency will require important changes in attitude on the part of both parties.

While I was a psychiatric resident in Baltimore, I had one year of analysis with Olive Cushing Smith. She was already of advanced years, aged seventy-three, having come to the practice of medicine in her forties and of psychoanalysis in her early fifties. Because I was leaving the city, the depth and intensity of the analysis was limited by our knowledge that the arrangement would be for a relatively short time. Nonetheless, I came to value the experience highly, and equally important, the qualities of the analyst as a person. Whenever I returned to visit the city, I used to visit Dr. Smith.

On the first two such occasions we met at her office, and I brought her up-to-date on the circumstances and events of my life. This was in keeping with, and a not unusual extension of, the therapeutic relationship which had existed during the active period of the psychoanalysis. The third visit, which took place about six years after I had left Baltimore, began in the same way. As I told her about what had happened to me in the interim, she listened with interest and with care. Then there was a pause, and she said: "But you haven't asked me what is happening to me." This was said with a smile, and not as a rebuke, but it did signal that our relationship was taking a new turn. It had not been appropriate for me to ask about her in the past, but clearly she felt that it now was. It was a Saturday morning, and she told me that it was in fact the final day of her practice. At the age of seventy-nine, after about twenty-five years of psychoanalytic work she was retiring. She went on to tell me how strange she felt to be doing so, but that it seemed to be the right time for a change. We discussed her feelings, including her pleasure that, by coincidence, I had come on that very day. There was only the slightest awkwardness about this shift in our relationship: mostly it felt both appropriate and satisfying to the two of us.

In the subsequent fifteen years, until her death, I visited her in her home another five or six times. She was always pleased to see me, and continued to follow with great interest the course of my career and my life. In turn I welcomed the increasing opportunity to give to her the friendship and interest and occasional companionship which were now, because of her advanced age and increasing physical limitations, so important to her.

When I had been the one who was more in need, and hence had more to receive than to give, she had given to me comfortably and easily. When it had been time for me to move on, she accepted that with comfort and grace. I felt her wish that I should grow free and independent. When eventually our positions were reversed by the passage of time, neither of us had difficulty in adapting to the change.

While the therapeutic relationship is being established the therapist must be careful not to adopt certain attitudes which will stand in the way of the patient's capacity to become self reliant. The silent, uncommunicative therapist will encourage in the patient's mind a sense of the great difference between them: that the patient is there to work, the therapist to observe and occasionally to comment. From this "superior" position he may indicate that it is his responsibility to prevent the patient from becoming too dependent. Therefore in order to avoid this the patient is to make all his own decisions and cannot expect the therapist to show him what he thinks is best for him. The opposite is true. This type of ungiving therapist induces a regressive attitude in both the rebellious and the compliant patient. The former will take offense and become unable to form a satisfactory working alliance with the therapist. The latter will be in awe of the therapist and consider himself fortunate to be cared for by such an accomplished person. This position is regressive: under the illusion that he is growing stronger, the patient is in fact become more infantile in the surrender of himself to the therapist. True growth involves an increase in *self*-esteem. That warm glow which comes from the adulation of another is, as we have seen in the case of James, a borrowed sense of well-being, and denotes neither stability nor strength.

The capacity of parents to allow their children to grow can be measured by how they deal with the thousands of decisions they must make throughout the years, revealing to what extent they truly wish the child ultimately to manage very well in the world without them.

So it is in psychotherapy. The patient who senses the therapist's wish for his growing independence and self-reliance is a patient who is very well treated. He will feel supported when he needs support, responded to when he requires a response. He will have the benefit of another person's point-of-view about people and events and feelings which will help him develop a sense of trust in his perception of reality. And he will feel that he is guided with a light hand, one which is ready to be taken gently away when he is no longer in need of it. These conclusions have not been drawn from what I was taught either in psychiatry or psychoanalysis. I learned, both from my own life and from my work with patients, that this is the case. Those, such as parents and teachers, who deal successfully with others who are dependent follow these principles intuitively. Whether dealing with my children, my students, or my patients, I have seen that this is what people require in order to become more self-reliant and independent.

Naturally, how the question of ending treatment is managed is always very revealing. The silent therapist may give the patient no more help in this matter than he has given in others. He may say: "I never tell my patients that therapy must terminate, as they will feel abandoned. I always leave it to them to make the decision as to whether they are ready to go." This apparently empathetic and democratic position may indeed mask just the opposite. It may represent the therapist's inability to do without the patient's attachment. It may be that the therapist is so comfortable with a symbiotic connection, one in which he is highly valued, that he prefers not to hurry the day of separation.

Margaret had been in psychoanalysis for five years. She knew that she was reaching a point of diminishing returns in the treatment, but no mention was made of when the analysis would end, and when she raised the question it was not discussed. She had finally begun to arrange further training and education which would give her new vocational opportunities. It seemed time, although it would be painful for her, to step away from the analysis and move out on her own. Finally, she said one day in the analysis: "I feel I have to stop within a few months, otherwise I will not be moving ahead." There was silence, then:

"Do you have to?" responded the analyst. Margaret had far too little help in bringing her treatment to an end. It was not her needs which were being served by the continuation of the treatment, but those of the therapist.

In life, the flow of the passing generations is built upon the principle of give and take: the strong, established generation gives both to the new, developing generation and to the old, diminishing generation. The ebb and flow, the interdependence of the two participants in the psychotherapeutic relationship reflect this very same principle. A psychotherapy in which one or both participants are largely lacking in generosity will be very limited in what it can achieve, but one which is characterized from the outset by generosity on the part of both therapist and patient will flourish and be highly productive.

8

THE THREE-HORSE CHARIOT
Examining and Understanding
the Therapeutic Relationship

MUCH or most of what I have described as being characteristic
of psychotherapy would apply to many kinds of psychotherapy. But there is one characteristic which sets apart psychoanalysis and psychoanalytically oriented psychotherapy; that
is, the attention paid, in the therapy, to the relationship between the patient and the therapist.

When I was a first-year resident in psychiatry, and was
struggling to get hold of some basic tenets of psychotherapy,
one of my supervisors put forward an analogy which I have
found useful ever since. "Psychotherapy," he said, "is like a
chariot which is being drawn by three horses. One is the past,
one is the present, and one is the therapeutic relationship. The
task of the therapist is to ensure that all three areas are attended to. If any of the horses gets too far ahead, or too far
behind, the chariot will not move well. Attention must always
be paid to each of the three."

Examination of, and discussion about the therapeutic relationship is a hallmark of insight-oriented psychotherapies.
Without this activity, an essential element would be missing.

Not only does this represent a difference which distinguishes this group of psychotherapies from others, but even more striking, it is a feature which separates these psychotherapies from almost all other human endeavors. No other vocations, including the professions, undertake, as part of the work itself, to carefully scrutinize and discuss what happens between the people who are working together. It is true that in some personal relationships between friends, spouses, or lovers, an examination of the relationship occurs, particularly when one or both of the participants have engaged in psychotherapy. It is also true that in many working situations provision is made for a periodic review of how the employee relates to his peers, his clients, or his employer. However, in each of these instances, such review is an extension of the basic relationship, and provides an evaluation of how things have been going. In psychotherapy, on the other hand, evaluation of the relationship of the two people working together is an indigenous ingredient of the work itself.

It is the responsibility of the therapist to set the background against which such an examination can occur. If the patient is knowledgeable about therapy, as for example, when he is in training to be a psychoanalyst, then the patient will *expect* this examination to be a part of the treatment. When the patient has had no previous knowledge of, or experience with therapy, he must be helped to see that this is an important and useful part of the process.

In some instances, a therapist may set out guidelines for the task ahead. So, when the agreement has been reached to work together, he might say: "We will talk about whatever interests you and is important to you: your thoughts, ideas, and dreams, what has happened in the past, what takes place in the present, and what happens between us." Or he may simply begin the therapy, leaving it to the patient to understand, as the work progresses, that all manner of things are the appropriate purview of the therapy. The patient may be surprised or shocked the first time the therapist focuses on something which has taken place between them. That may be the time the therapist chooses to indicate the significance of this part of the work.

A caricature of how one deals with such matters might be exemplified by the therapist who, when examining the relationship, always finds the patient at fault. He might suggest to him, when he was late for an appointment because a flowerpot fell on his head, that his unconscious resistance to therapy had caused him to engineer the event, to avoid some of the pain which treatment brings.

In fact, there are difficulties which must be faced by both parties when they attempt to examine their relationship. In the first place, whatever happens between them, however insignificant it may appear, must be scrutinized. Then, it must be recognized that superimposed on the natural interaction that takes place between any two people, are the distortions which *each* brings to the relationship because of his residual neurotic problems. Transference and countertransference will of necessity arise in the therapeutic relationship because of the interdependence which I have described in chapter 7. It is presumed that those distortions that the patient projects onto the therapist (transference), are greater in degree and more frequently manifested than those that the therapist projects onto the patient (countertransference). If this is not the case then little useful therapy will occur; the same will be true if the therapist is arrogant and assumes that distortions are produced only by the patient. The therapy will also be severely limited if the therapist believes that, although they are both responsible for distortions and problems that arise between them, only those pertaining to the patient are to be brought forward and discussed. This latter stance, where the therapist takes the position that if he were to admit he was at fault, it would get in the way of the patient's treatment, is paternalistic, and unfortunately is not unknown in therapy.

This same misguided attitude is shown by the parent who will never admit to a child that the fault between them has been his. This leads, in the younger child, to idealization of the parent, a state which *may* never end. Often, in the older child, or when that child has become an adult, it leads to disillusionment and rejection of the parent, his values, and his life.

Margaret (whom I mentioned in chapter 7) whose therapist was reluctant for her to leave, was in psychoanalysis for a period of five years. She was intelligent, a housewife and mother, and a college graduate. When the treatment began, her three children were all in school. She had decided, with her husband's concurrence, that it was best for the children if she did not return to work until they were all of upper high-school age. Hence these years seemed suitable for her psychoanalysis. She had no problems or symptoms of a serious nature. Rather, she was periodically unhappy and anxious, and recognized that there was too much of her that was unexpressed and unfulfilled.

Margaret had always been cautious with new people, so she was cautious and even suspicious in the early months of the analysis. She wondered about her analyst's general trustworthiness. She was basically rather competitive, particularly with men, and feared that the analyst would take advantage of her vulnerable and, should she become so, dependent position. Before long, these suspicious attitudes began to change. The analyst was friendly and reliable. He was patient and attentive. He did not say much, or explain much, but he listened well. As the months passed, she trusted him more and more. By virtue of this accepting, tolerant attitude on the analyst's part, Margaret became not only trusting but very dependent upon the analyst. Weekend breaks were met with considerable diffi-

culty, vacations with much more. In the early years the analyst's manifest consideration of how badly such separations made her feel was a help, and she was deeply grateful for his consideration.

She did have one reservation. Whenever difficulties arose between them, only her contribution was examined. The implicit message in this was: "I am the analyst. Because of my own analysis and my experience, what I contribute is normal and realistic. Against this backdrop the psychoneurotic (transference) distortions which you contribute can be examined." He was never at fault. Whenever she accused him of any limitation he became self-justifying and angry. Whether his sensitivity, his memory, or his interpretation was in question, he always, one way or another, rejected the implication that he might be at fault.

Margaret correctly understood herself to be in a very vulnerable position. She learned that she could not seriously challenge the analyst, because if she did he would either be hurt, and withdraw, or be defensive and attacking of her. In either event she would lose his approval, of which she felt very much in need. In the beginning of the analysis she feared that should she offend him too deeply he would ask her to leave treatment. Later she saw that this would not happen, but that if she were critical of him she would lose that approbation which felt like the most helpful and nourishing part of her relationship with him. She was very conflicted within herself on this point: on the one hand she elevated him to a position of great power and intelligence; on the other hand she recognized his immaturity in being unable to be criticized or found to be at fault.

Margaret learned to get along. In time she kept her doubts and reservations to herself, and did not raise them in the analysis. Fortunately, she had a close friend in whom she could confide these matters. This took the pressure off and allowed her, within the therapeutic situation, to be perceived as a sufficiently compliant and grateful patient. Within herself she came to know that the analyst, however long and complete his own psychoanalysis, remained a basically defensive man who had to be right and needed to be admired.

When five years had elapsed, Margaret knew that she was ready to terminate the treatment, and several months after she had announced this decision, the analysis ended. She recognized that she had derived some benefit from the treatment but was disappointed that it had been marred by such a serious flaw. As the ensuing years passed, she was able gradually to undo much of the overdependency which had been allowed to flower in the analysis. She recognized more and more the limits of the analyst and realized with regret that her treatment could have been much more valuable had her relationship with the analyst been handled differently.

Examining and understanding the therapeutic relationship is one of the most important dimensions of insight-oriented psychotherapy. But what I have learned is that when the therapist, in effect, leaves himself out of it, great opportunities are lost. It was not until years later that Margaret was able to understand fully how twisted a position her therapist had taken and how adversely this had affected the analysis.

Sometimes the errors of the therapist can be helpful when they are confronted with the patient.

I had been on sabbatical leave for a month when I received a letter from Phyllis. She had been in psychotherapy with me for three years, having come because of anxiety attacks, dizziness, and the fear that she would pass out on the street. Her symptoms had cleared up, and she had made great strides in improving her life with her family, for it was there that the conflicts lay that were at the source of her symptoms. I had seen her for the last time just before going away. In the letter she told me that our final session had been a terrible one.

"I have never had one like it," she wrote. "You made a serious mistake and I didn't correct you. You said that my sister, whose husband died last year, was unusually unkind to me, favoring my husband, because she was jealous that my husband was still alive.

But she isn't. John is a very poor husband to me. She has a lover whom she had for years before her husband died, and now she's happier than ever. She certainly doesn't envy me, and her bad behavior to me cannot be explained that way."

I arranged to meet with her when I was next in the city. She told me that she had written to me, for the first time, with great difficulty. She had a headache following her last visit with me. She tore up three letters, but finally posted one. As soon as she put it in the mailbox her headache disappeared.

"You are entirely right. I didn't have all the facts, and what I said was wrong," I said.

"I couldn't let it end that way," she replied.

"How does it feel now?"

"Just fine. I am glad we got it right."

I have pointed out, thus far, that it is helpful and important for therapist and patient to discuss all that happens between them within the context of the therapy. In addition, there is often another opportunity which will present itself, and which can be very productive, and that is to deal with anything that has to do with the relationship of the two people should they meet away from the consulting room. Such contacts arise more frequently in the case of candidates in training to be psychoanalysts, for often the analyst and the analysand might work in the same hospital or university and find some overlap in their professional or social lives. In some instances the two people might feel they have to decide which one of them should attend a social function to which they have both been invited. The reason for this would be to avoid "flooding" the treatment with too much material about the therapist. Very often such a position has been adhered to by therapists to an unnecessary and even ludicrous degree; however, it is true that sometimes it is best to avoid prolonged social contact between the two people.

A patient and I discovered, in the first few months of his analysis, that a mutual acquaintance had invited us both, with our spouses, to a small dinner party. The matter was discussed in the analysis.

"I found out something today that made me feel rather uncomfortable," said Paul.

"What was that?" I asked.

"You and your wife have been invited to dinner on Saturday night at the Johnsons' house. So have we."

"Oh, I didn't know you were invited as well. What are your feelings about it?"

"They are hard for me to define clearly. All I know is that I became uncomfortable as soon as I learned about it."

"What do you think it might be?"

"It is something to do with sitting down for a couple of hours in that setting, where there will be only a few of us. Also, your wife will be there. It all feels too exposed, considering we have been working together for only a few months. Perhaps I shouldn't feel this way, but I do."

"It is natural to feel this way. It would expose you to a great deal about me personally, and it is probably too early for that to be helpful."

"What should we do about it?"

"I suggest that it would be easier for our work if one of us did not accept the invitation. Later on in the analysis it will not pose the same problem. How would that solution feel to you?"

"I would be relieved."

That was the solution on that occasion. In later years, because there was some overlap in our professional and social lives, there were many similar occasions. By then we felt comfortable in having much more social exposure to one another. In fact those later occasions provided useful material to be subsequently examined, with good result, in the analysis.

This seems a justified position to take: the patient was just getting to know the analyst, just beginning to try to trust him.

Several hours spent at the same dinner table, with spouses present, would have been out of keeping with the developing relationship. The following is a different kind of example with another patient.

After two years of psychotherapy, Martin and I found ourselves at the same cocktail reception. When we first met, early in the evening, Martin felt shy and awkward. Fortunately, I felt and behaved comfortably and that put him at his ease. We chatted briefly.

"How are you this evening?" I enquired.

"Fine," Martin replied. "How about yourself?"

"Very well. What do you think of this crowd?"

"Well," he answered, "it's not what I prefer. As I've often told you, I find such gatherings meaningless. How about yourself?"

"I feel the same, though it's good to see those few people I like and don't often see."

"I agree. Well, I'll see you later."

"Yes, See you."

Later in the evening Martin saw me a few times in the crowd. He found himself making many observations about myself and my wife, who seemed to be enjoying one another's company. We talked quietly and at length to a few people, rather than circulating and being in touch with many people. By chance I ended up for a while in the company of Martin's wife, who later commented upon my style of dress, my way of speaking, and the content of my conversation.

After the initial meeting, Martin felt less awkward; and yet there remained something different in the situation from the usual social meeting with a friend or acquaintance. Somehow Martin was always aware of where I was in the room, and because of the intense feelings he felt toward me, I seemed larger than life. Martin's attention was repeatedly drawn to me and his curiosity to observe more about me was quite evident within himself.

The party was on Saturday evening. The next time we met was at the session on Monday morning. Martin sat down, and felt the awkwardness once again. He was not sure where to begin.

"*It was unusual for us to find ourselves at the same social function, as we did Saturday,*" I said. "*What feelings did you have about the evening?*" Martin was relieved that the ice had been broken in this way.

"*I had many feelings,*" he replied, "*both during the evening and since.*"

"*Why don't you tell me about them?*" I suggested. Martin did so, and most of the session was taken up with looking at Martin's feelings. Most of them had been positive: he was glad that I had taken the initiative in talking with him. He liked my quiet social manner. He approved of the look of my wife, and the way she and I seemed to get along together. Some reactions were negative, or potentially so. He feared that I might be someone who drank too much. He had been afraid in the beginning that I might behave toward him in a superior or all-knowing or even condescending way, but this did not happen. He was worried that he might have appeared to me or others to be as awkward as he felt, and was relieved to learn from me that this had not been the case. He had wanted me to meet his wife, and we discussed both his relief and his concerns over this meeting.

Not only that session, but several subsequent sessions included material from that meeting. Whereas Martin had felt diffident at first, especially in discussing his reservations about me in quite personal matters, he found that it became increasingly easy to be frank, as I showed a full willingness to, and even interest in, discussing such areas. The most important fact for Martin was that whatever matter he raised, I did not become self-justifying or defensive. All aspects of our meeting seemed open to evaluation without the fear that I might take offense. In this way a great deal which was valuable had been introduced into the therapy. Many feelings of an intensely personal nature between Martin and myself were able to be discussed. All of this set a precedent for the handling of such matters when they arose later in the therapy.

The three most important aspects of what happened with Martin were the result of how our meeting was handled. The first was that when it occurred, it was treated in a natural way, as would be the case of any social situation. The second was that I initiated and encouraged, in the next therapeutic session, a full discussion of the meeting and the feelings which it had evoked. The third was that I was not evasive or defensive about negative thoughts and feelings that the patient had expressed. In fact I showed myself to be equally interested in hearing negative or positive feelings about myself.

Although discussing such matters in therapy is of the greatest importance, some therapists do not do so. It is principally two kinds of feelings in a therapist which keep him from exploring such material. The first, based upon uncertainty and self-doubt, operates in the following way: the therapist feels, "I cannot ask the patient what he felt when we met, for if I suggest that he has significant feelings toward me, he might say, or he might think that I am too taken up with my own importance." In fact the therapeutic situation is such as to stimulate strong reactions in any patient, and such an attitude on the part of the therapist is false modesty, which stems from his wish to be the most important, and his unresolved fear that he is not.

The second, based upon grandiosity, might be illustrated by the following thoughts on the part of the therapist: "I will not deign to discuss what the patient felt about me; both he and I are aware that I am always uppermost in his thoughts, and since his feelings of admiration and affection for me are so strong, it would be in poor taste to draw undue attention to them." In fact, in this latter instance, what the therapist is least prepared to hear is that the patient has reservations about him. Like Margaret, the patient will detect such an attitude, when it resides in the therapist, and will learn to keep his negative feelings to himself. This will result in a most serious limitation of what can be accomplished.

It is because of feelings such as these that it is of help for a therapist to have himself undergone therapy or psychoanalysis. For having come to terms with his own feelings of both inferiority and grandiosity, it is then more likely that he could invite and permit the fullest exploration by the patient of all manner of feelings about himself. A psychoanalyst will have had a personal analysis, as it is a required part of his training. Many, but not all other therapists have chosen to have some personal treatment.

Why is it of such importance that the therapy include an examination of the relationship between the two participants?· Because the therapeutic situation naturally magnifies all of those feelings which the patient has in more ordinary or normal relationships. This magnification allows both patient and therapist to see more clearly how the patient's thoughts and feelings tend to work. Also, one of the principal ways in which the therapist will be helpful will be through his enabling the patient to see reality more clearly, both the reality of the world around him, and of his inner world. Most of what the therapist learns *about* the patient he learns *from* the patient, so that the therapist must work hard to translate the patient's view into a realistic view of the world. But what happens between the two of them is not merely reported to the therapist by the patient; indeed, this is one portion of the patient's life experience to which the therapist has also been witness, whether it is outside or inside the consulting room.

"You are more quiet than usual today," said the therapist. The first few minutes of the session had been mainly filled with silences.

"I don't seem to be able to get started on anything," responded the patient.

"Has something been bothering you—perhaps about the therapy, or perhaps about me?"

"I don't think so," the patient replied. "Well, there is something I have been thinking about."

"What is that?"

"I don't know whether or not you saw me yesterday when you passed in the lobby after our session. I nodded at you, but you seemed to look right through me."

"I'm sorry," said the therapist, "in fact I did not see you."

"You did look somewhat harassed."

"I was late, and was rushing off to see someone. Somehow I didn't see you."

"I thought that was probably the case, but I wasn't sure."

"What thoughts did you have about it later?"

"I kept thinking about it during the evening. I was hurt by what you told me yesterday, that is, that I had treated you meanly the day before. I knew you were right. Somewhere underneath I had hoped to hurt you. But I didn't like being confronted with what I had done."

"I could see that you were hurt as I was speaking."

"It's true. And I was afraid that you were so angry with me that you snubbed me in the lobby. And yet at the same time I knew you wouldn't do that to me. I did feel that you had been angry with me for what I had done."

"It is true," replied the therapist, "I had been angry. But once I told you about it, and you had agreed with my view of what had happened, I was no longer angry. I would not deliberately snub you."

"I really know that," said the patient, "and yet somehow I wasn't entirely certain."

When checking is done in this way, openly with the patient, it can be of exceptional value in helping him improve his ability to assess reality.

HAVING AND NOT HAVING: LEARNING TO SHARE

Clara had been in analysis with me for several months: she had spent
most of the time in silence. Every once in a while she would become
angry, accusing me of having the wrong attitude toward her.

"You are impossible to talk to," she said.

"Why is that?"

"I make no contact with you. You sit there staring at me, like a
scientist looking down his microscope at a specimen, or examining a
bug on the end of a pin. It is inhuman, and it turns me off."

Clara was complaining that although I was able to observe her and
work with her, I was not able to give her the feeling of sharing that
she required before she could open up to me. It took further months
before she finally felt that she could trust me enough to tell me what
lay within herself. That only came when she found me more able to
share some of my own personal feelings with her.

The question of having and not having comes unavoidably
into the therapeutic relationship, but first I would like to discuss this subject in a more general sense.

We are born wanting everything, or so it seems. But everyone can't have everything, and thus many problems are
created. Learning to live in the world requires doing without,
or sharing, or waiting for what we want. A very large part of
what happens in useful psychotherapy will be around this
subject: for not having is one of the principal sources of pain in
people, and a good psychotherapist will try to assuage that
pain by helping the patient to see, accept, and work within the
limits that reality imposes.

The commonest reason that people come for psychotherapy
is that they have sustained some loss. That loss may be dealt

with only briefly by the therapist, who will encourage the patient to accept and adjust to it. Or it may be the means by which the patient is precipitated into sorely needed long-term therapy, in which case much time will be spent in his treatment learning about the difficulties caused by losses and unsatisfied desires.

When the patient comes to therapy, there are several tasks which will be required of him and the therapist with regard to the question of having and not having. The first is to acquire some awareness of what his needs are and why they are not being met. The second is to differentiate between those wishes which might conceivably be fulfilled, and those which are unrealistic. A third task is to understand the parts played both by the patient and by others in his life in establishing and maintaining an unsatisfying situation. Other tasks are to determine how the patient might arrange for his needs to be more fully satisfied, and to develop his judgment about such matters, so that in time he will make better choices of friends, jobs, and recreational activities.

When we think about having and not having, we are looking at things, in the first instance, from the patient's point of view. One unfortunate assumption which is sometimes made in psychotherapy is that the most important objective is the satisfaction of the patient's wishes. Such a direction is not just unrealistic and myopic, but it is self-defeating. No one can take only his own needs into account and expect to have a basically satisfying life.

The earliest lessons about not having must come in the family, and later from society. As the infant becomes a child, and later an adult, he must increasingly take into account the needs of others. If he has been spoiled into thinking that, for a lifetime, only *his* needs really matter, then he will be a person whose character is impaired. In the most extreme case we will have someone whose psychopathy is such that all attempts to concern him about the welfare of others fails. Or, if the degree of impairment is more moderate, we will have someone who is manipulative or narcissistic in ways which only show up under some circumstances but who, sooner or later, becomes a major disappointment to the people close to him.

It is a matter of opinion as to the degree to which one may be born destined to be deficient in the area of concern for others, and the degree to which it arises out of life's experiences. My own belief is that what happens *after* birth is infinitely more important than that which is constitutional. There are, it is true, a very few people who seem from birth to be unable to concern themselves with the wishes or needs of others. Probably they are people who are born with greater than average needs, and are difficult to satisfy, even with the very best parenting, but they are a very small minority. A much larger group consists of those who have not, within the family and within society, been sufficiently required to take into account any point of view or any need other than their own.

At times I have been confronted with evidence of uncaring behavior, and it has been necessary to decide what that behavior says about the patient.

"I am ashamed of what I did to you," said Carla.

"I'm glad you are, because if you weren't it would say something much worse about you," I replied. "Why do you think you did it?"

"I don't know," she said. "I found you were very vulnerable in the situation, and I couldn't help but test you—give you a hard time. I had to see what you would do. What you did was confront me with what I was doing. I feel mean, the way I often have, over the years. What does it say about me?"

"I'm not certain. I think it says that you can be mean when you need to test someone. It could say that you don't give a damn about

anyone and, once you feel safe in doing so, you get away with as much as you can."

"Which do you think it is?"

"I think it is testing. It is defensive. It is your way of seeing whether, if you hurt someone, he will turn against you and prove what you most fear—that he is really not interested in you. I think it is something that will drop away in time. I hope I am right."

In this case it turned out to be so. Carla, as she came to know me better, trusted me more and showed me that basically she cared a great deal for others.

In the psychotherapeutic situation all of this is of the utmost importance. In the first instance, as I have already described, it is the business of the therapist to explore with the patient what he wants, what he needs, and what he has and has not. In the second instance, the therapist wants to know whether the patient can be concerned about others and their welfare. Since this characteristic is an issue so central to the quality of every person's life and as it is one of the most significant requisites of growing up, then in therapy much attention must be paid by both therapist and patient to this subject.

Helen's chronic unhappiness was not able to be changed in psychotherapy. As I demonstrated with an earlier example in chapter 7 she carried with her at all times a sense of grave injustice about what the world had done to her.

She was born intelligent and energetic in a family of striving, restless, unhappy people. The problems of her parents and siblings had always intruded upon her, so there had never been a stable and satisfying period in her life. She completed a university education and became a competent member of her profession. She was almost always unhappy.

Some years of psychotherapy revealed the roots of this unhappiness, as well as the nature of her attitudes. It was not that Helen did not care for and about others—she did, and to a painful degree. But she could not escape the conviction that no one really cared for her.

That she did not marry was a crushing humiliation to her. Efforts on my part to show her that she could, being single, make a very good life for herself, were met with furious rejection. She responded with intense anger to each disappointment she experienced in connection with her needs and her preferences. It all felt intolerably unfair. For years she was depressed as a result of these feelings. Later she became very blaming of others rather than of herself, and constantly attacked the world around her for what it had done to her.

For a while it seemed as though psychotherapy would make a very great difference to Helen. She was at times more satisfied, even mildly elated when things were going well. But in the end she would always revert to an inflamed rage against the world in general and me in particular, for continuing to deprive her of those things she most wanted: a home, a circle of friends, a family to love.

"How dare you suggest that I should settle for so little?" she demanded.

"Because if you do not become better at settling for what you have, you will be forever miserable. You spoil what you have by demanding that you must have much more."

"What do you know about it? Life is easy for you. You have what you want, so it is simple for you to waste my time and my money telling me to accept less than you would ever be willing to accept. Why won't you help me in some way?"

"I do what I can."

"No you don't. If you wanted to help more, you would surely find some way to do so."

Helen continued to ask why, despite her best efforts, life passed her by, and why, as hard as she tried, she could not improve her lot. No answer seemed satisfactory either to her or to the therapist. Somehow this rather attractive and able person always broadcast her anger and her discontent to others. So, although she was able to know and work with many people, she was unable to attract and hold people in intimate friendships. For this the world was never to be forgiven, an attitude which severely impeded and limited the therapy.

Helen cared about others, but felt so deprived at all times that her caring feelings could not surface. She would not intentionally hurt someone else. It is rather that she always felt so hurt by what she saw as the unconcern of others, that her own discomfort became a preoccupation. Some others who may seem similar to Helen are in fact rather different: they also put themselves first, but they find this easier to do, because deep feelings of concern for others do not exist.

Rachael was handsome and intelligent and, as a result, had usually been able to get what she wanted. Her early life had been difficult, marked by numerous losses, and rather than weakening her, this had toughened her. She had developed social skills to a very high level, being able to please and flatter others where necessary. She projected an impression of enlightened agreeableness, but this was deceptive. In fact she was agreeable only insofar as it would get her what she wanted and what she felt she deserved.

Rachael entered treatment only because of a loss in her life. The death of her fiancé enraged her. It interfered with her life's plan. Her rage, with some depression, was accompanied by a high sense of self-justified indignation.

"When he was ill for those several months I sat with him, but I couldn't talk to him."

"Why?"

"I couldn't forgive him for becoming fatally ill when we had all those plans."

"Did you feel sorry for him?"

"Yes, but I must admit my anger was the stronger. He knew it, too. In the end I hated to go and see him in the hospital because he

could tell that, whatever I said to the contrary, I couldn't forgive him."

Therapy helped her to understand the original roots of her sense of being deprived; and to see how she had determined that nothing would stand in the way of her getting whatever she desired. It allowed her to recognize the sources from which had arisen her single-minded pursuit of security and even power in her relations with others. In time, these discoveries diminished the anger and depression, and allowed her to resume the previous course of her life.

What therapy did not accomplish was to make Rachael a basically more caring person. She left treatment feeling grateful and improved. But the years that followed continued to be characterized by a "me first" attitude. The quality of her principal relationships remained fundamentally self-serving, something that will not change.

"We have done what we can," I said.

"I appreciate your help. How do you think I will make out?"

"You will see to it that you make out very well. Others close to you will benefit from your talents and energy. Unfortunately, in time they will learn about your selfishness, and they will be disappointed that that is how you are."

Rachael remains a manipulative person. As long as things go her way, and they usually do because of her talent for arranging life to her liking, she is manifestly kindly, friendly, and warm. As soon as something stands in her way she becomes cool and demanding, shifting her attention and affection to where it will do the most good for her. And always the message is the same: "What is good for me is best, what is bad for me is intolerable."

Helen and Rachael were helped in psychotherapy to a limited degree only. Many other patients are helped much more in the area of having and not having because they have more flexibility than existed in these two people. The large majority of patients do find, through the understanding which psychotherapy provides, that they are able to be more accepting of what life offers and what is beyond their reach. They also discover how they stand in the way of their own success, either with people or in their work. Modifying their attitude toward sharing and then their behavior allows them to achieve and obtain more of what they wish for.

Thus far I have explained some of the ways in which psychotherapy can be of use in this matter of having and not having, but there is one more way, and that is, as I mentioned earlier, when the subject of having or not having arises within the context of the therapeutic relationship. When it does, as it will frequently, it offers the patient an excellent opportunity gradually to see and understand his needs and the extent to which they can be met by someone who is important to him. For example, what is the therapist prepared to give to the patient—how much time, how much interest, how much affection? What will the therapist demand from the patient— how much energy, how much money, how much compliance?

Every patient in any form of intensive psychotherapy develops strong feelings about where he stands with the therapist. At one stage of therapy most patients want so much to be the chief or even exclusive concern of the therapist that somehow they imagine that their treatment is the principal function in his life. Anyone who works intensively for some time with a therapist will become aware of his wish, even his need, to come first with the therapist. This will not be a simple matter of intellectual understanding. It will be a matter of the greatest emotional import, occasioning the strongest of feelings. The patient may become really depressed at the time of his own or the therapist's vacation. He may be terribly envious of other patients he meets, or resentful of friends or relatives of the therapist whom he hears about, being jealous of their relationship with the therapist. All of this is painful but it is highly important grist for the therapeutic mill.

Within the therapeutic relationship, all of this must be handled with the greatest care and skill by the therapist. The patient must learn that the therapist cares about him, uniquely but not exclusively. By understanding that every human relationship is different from every other one he can retain the sense of specialness that all of us seek. On the other hand, he must come to grips with the fact that, just as his mother needed to give some of her love and attention elsewhere, the therapist also has other concerns and attachments. In psychotherapy there is unavoidably enacted within the relationship the patient's wish to have all things and all people—exclusively and instantly. The careful, understanding attention given to these powerful feelings by the therapist will lead in time to a softening of and a greater control of those feelings on the part of the patient. Of all that takes place in psychotherapy, nothing is of greater importance than the experience, the recognition, and the resolution of such feelings.

For the therapist, it is easy to err on either side of this question. On the one hand, he may, wanting to gratify the patient who has been frustrated excessively, allow the patient to feel that he has the exclusive love and special concern of the therapist. When this is carried to excess, we may find that this fantasy is never resolved, and that the patient ends the treatment still enveloped and basking in the glow of the therapist's special love and admiration. On the other hand, the therapist may repeat, within the therapeutic relationship, the rejecting position of the parents, never being quite satisfied with the patient, who in turn is always trying to gain the therapist's approval. Somewhere between these two extremes lies the most desirable position: one in which the patient feels cared for and uniquely appreciated for himself, and where, at the same time, he knows the reality of his importance in the life of the therapist. Recognizing and accepting such a position will be a major step in the growth and maturation of the patient.

Out of the having and not having arise some of the most difficult feelings with which people have to contend: jealousy and envy. We are jealous of the closeness that others have with one another. We envy others for all the things which they may have, which we would like to have. This is an area of feelings which always needs to be dealt with in the therapy. Some people can appreciate what they have, or what they have been given. Being able to give anything to others, including gratitude, is one most significant measure of a person's character. One cannot give if one has not been given to. One is not generous if one feels that one has always been and is being deprived by others.

Within the therapeutic relationship it will be of great importance whether each of the two people can give and be grateful, and accept from one another. For the patient, if the experience is a good one, it may be one of the only times he has experienced such giving. As for the therapist, although he must do most of the giving, he should also expect something in return from the patient.

And so learning to share, most particularly to share good feelings, is central to any successful psychotherapy. That good experience within the therapy leads to change in the relationships of the patient, first with the therapist, and then with others out in his world. This is the source of the greatest pleasures which can exist between people. When it occurs within the therapeutic experience, the greatest satisfaction will exist for both patient and therapist, for the therapy will have achieved one of its most important goals.

9

THE INNER REALITY
Feelings

HUMAN beings' feelings or emotions are the richest part of their heritage. These are the best part of our animal ancestry, creating a colorful fabric in which each of our lives is woven like a thread. Feelings are much older than those relative newcomers, thinking and reasoning. Unfortunately for us, technological societies in recent times have overvalued the power of reason. Of course our frontal cortex is important, for it has allowed us to adapt to all kinds of conditions and circumstances and enabled us to control our world and our destinies in marvelous ways. But reason is not enough for good living. We are provided with a rich panoply of potential feelings, and if we are to flourish, we must use them and experience them.

The development of psychiatry and psychoanalysis, part art, part science, has helped us learn about feelings at the deepest level. This has been the principal contribution of psychoanalysis to the understanding of people. Sadly, psychiatry, psychoanalysis, and the other helping professions have fallen into some serious errors in the course of their development. We have become so enamored of our theories that we have taken them to be as real as rocks and trees and clouds.

They are not; they are only theories. The words that we use in order to make the discussion of such matters clearer and simpler have instead made it more obscure and complex. Terms such as *ego, id, borderline personality, resistance*, and *narcissistic character* were not known to Homer, Milton, Shakespeare, or Dickens. Yet somehow these authors conveyed their sense of the human condition with extraordinary authenticity, as did those who wrote the Old and New Testaments. Each of us feels the veracity of the themes and the emotions and the values described in such works. One cannot say as much for psychiatric reports and case studies.

The essential work of psychotherapy is the understanding of the feelings of people, and what they do to cope with and handle those feelings. People are afraid of feelings—that has always been the case. They are afraid of the pain that feelings bring. So, often without being aware of it, they find a variety of ways to avoid that pain. None of these ways lead to a good result, for that avoidance brings unhappiness and dissatisfaction.

Some feelings are basic to our existence, such as love and hate, anxiety, anger, and fear. Some are defensive, attempting to make us feel better, but bringing their own set of problems, for example, omnipotence, arrogance, and the denial of reality. Some, such as loyalty, ambition, and generosity represent character values which have a profound effect upon the quality of our lives. Others are at the core of our existence as separate individuals; these include our conflicting needs to attach to others and yet to be separate and autonomous.

People in technological societies have developed their own way out of the dilemma that feelings present: they favor intellect, convincing themselves that thinking can take over from feeling. This does not work. For reason, as powerful as it can be, must give over to the emotions, which in evolutionary terms long preceded it. In the course of psychotherapy, including psychoanalysis, the minds of therapist and patient struggle to understand the feelings which bubble up from inside the patient. Such feelings give color and texture and excitement to living. An informed life, informed about feelings, can be a richer life, as it leads a person to a greater understanding of, and hence comfort and pleasure with the human condition.

Engaging in psychotherapy is one way of helping us to know about our feelings, but it is not the only way. Introspection helps, as does the discussion of ourselves and others with trustworthy friends. Reading helps—not so much the reading of psychological treatises as the reading of the great novelists, dramatists, and poets. The conflicts of Hamlet and how they affect him are important not because they illustrate the significance of the Oedipus complex, but because they show the kind of torture that a person can feel when caught in the currents of emotions about mother, father, and friends. Robert Burns's compassionate discourse "To a Mouse," which he addresses to a "fellow mortal," will teach us much about our attitudes to human kindness and humility. Observing other people can help us to know ourselves and our feelings. It helps us to counter our natural tendency to deny what people are really like—allowing us to *really* see them and what they do and to *really* hear what they say. A great deal can be learned about feelings from watching and listening to children—not discounting what they say, but taking it seriously, even literally. "Out of the mouths of babes" is likely to come more truth and more frankness than out of the mouths of adults who have been conditioned for so long to heed the prohibitions of society.

Each of these ways of learning about feelings has a place in understanding ourselves. None of them, including psychotherapy, is the best or sole way of determining what lies within us. Psychotherapy, however, has a particular advantage, for seeking the truth within ourselves is most readily accomplished in the company of a concerned, informed, and helpful person.

WHAT HAPPENS TO FEELINGS?

Animals, other than humans, are not taught, except when they live with humans, to curb their feelings. A dog may be taught that he has to be quiet even when he feels joyous or angry or afraid, but for the most part he will express his feelings as they arise. Certainly this is the natural way of animals when they are away from people. People are taught, as members of societies, what is expected of them with respect to feelings, and they are taught such lessons beginning in early infancy and throughout their lives. People cannot only feel feelings, they can be aware of, think about, and discuss feelings. So curbing their feelings may not only restrict their awareness of them, it may also restrict their ability to express them. Even further, they may be taught to curb the realization that they even *have* certain feelings. All of these aspects of the training of people by society have important, even profound effects upon them. When members of complex technological societies are in touch with members of more traditional societies who have not been curbed in the same way, they are struck by how much those people differ from themselves.

Anthropologist Marjorie Shostak interviewed a fifty-year-old woman, whom she called Nisa, one of the !Kung people in the Kalahari area of Africa. Nisa was not only extraordinarily outspoken about her feelings, but she was also strikingly free of any view that she "should not be feeling" what she was feeling. She spoke freely and openly about her great jealousy toward her younger brother, and how she wanted the milk from their mother's breasts which he got and she no longer did. She told how angry she was when others had food, especially meat from a hunt, when she did not, and how she would tell them that she wanted and expected some of that food. She told how she resented and fought the demands of others that she felt were unreasonable. All of this was expressed without regret or guilt or hesitation, since she had not been trained to believe that it was wrong to have and express such feelings.

Therapists in our society deal with people who have had a lifetime of training against the free expression and even recognition of feelings. There are general influences of this kind which exist for all of us, and which are mediated through laws and traditions and mores of our district, our religion, our country, and our educational and vocational institutions. Then there are more specific influences from within our own families starting with the fears and prejudices and even irrationalities of the people who rear us.

Marjorie grew up with a psychotic mother (chapter 5). Her greatest pleasure was in writing poetry—her mother's greatest pleasure was in harassing, even torturing her daughter. One result of this was that Marjorie threw all of her poems into the furnace so that her mother would no longer be able to mock and taunt her for what she had written. In the first few years of therapy Marjorie was terrified to find out what she thought and felt. Her sadistic mother had programmed her not to feel what she really did feel, and not to know what her feelings really were. She had enormous guilt about her entirely justified hatred of her mother, who had not only abused her, but who had trained her to believe that she must be wrong, even evil, to have any such feelings toward the person most closely related to her. She believed that she was monstrous for what she felt, although what she felt was, in a sensitive and caring person, the inevitable result of the ways in which she had been treated.

Sometimes patients cannot sort out what it is that they feel, and what has come from others near them that they have accepted automatically as being the way they feel.

"I can't believe that I have such awful feelings," said Barbara.

"Which ones?" I asked.

"My resentment of my mother. My anger with my husband. My relief that I am so much better off than my brother."

"Why can't you believe it?"

"It doesn't seem right, they are such selfish feelings."

"Your mother led you to believe that, so you have tried your best to follow her directions."

"That's true. It all seems so disloyal."

"Your mother taught you that not to love and appreciate her was disloyal—and that there is no more despicable act than disloyalty. Yet you merely feel toward her what she deserved and earned. The same is the case with respect to your husband and brother."

"How can I feel that way?"

"Because you are you and not your mother. You have just begun to permit yourself to be as different from her as you really are."

Sometimes in therapy it takes a very long period of work before the patient is able to see and acknowledge what her own spontaneous, natural, and true feelings really are. This is because the mental mechanisms whereby the patient has kept her feelings out of her awareness are so strong. The patient has long used *denial* to keep from facing the feelings inside herself, because of the prohibitions that society has somehow conveyed to her. She may be partly or vaguely or sometimes aware of that which she has denied. When she is aware of the denied feelings, then we say that they are in her *conscious* mind. When they are temporarily out of her awareness, but can be brought to mind by an effort of her will, we say that they are in the *preconscious* part of her mind. When they have been relegated to that part of her mind where she does not have access to them and cannot bring them into awareness, we say that they are in the *unconscious* part of her mind. In this latter instance, a kind of forgetting has taken place, an active and yet unaware act that we call *repression*. All of those mental activities which keep feelings out of awareness or even totally out of consciousness have to be circumvented in the therapy. For the patient will pay a serious price if her feelings continue be to forgotten or denied.

The most usual price is a symptom of some kind, usually pain or discomfort of one form or another. One patient has anxiety attacks, another depression, another palpitations, another abdominal pain. The suppression of feelings also results in the constriction of the patient's personality. She does not have the degrees of freedom which she would otherwise have, as the feelings which need to be avoided are always threatening her, and she instinctively walks gingerly to avoid bumping into them. It is this last situation which gives people a chronic feeling of frustration or even alienation, a sense of being always held back or thwarted from within—unfulfilled, undeveloped, unnatural, and incomplete. In such instances successful therapy can lead to profound changes in the patient's personality.

Phyllis came for treatment after months of evaluation by her family physician and by a neurosurgeon. She had been plagued with dizziness which made her afraid that she would pass out in the street; she had never done so, but was always afraid that this would occur.

Phyllis was a successful artisan, highly respected in her field. She loved her work and thought that she loved her family. However, she had feelings from a generation earlier that she had never faced, never acknowledged, let alone accepted.

"I don't know how I had gone on so long that way," she later told me.

"You were under tremendous pressure all the time," I replied.

"Why was I so nice all the time?" she wanted to know.

"The main cause of that was that it was demanded by your mother. She quickly brought you to heel if ever you displayed any negative feelings, most particularly toward her. Even now, when she is very elderly and lives thousands of miles away, she can make you feel guilty with how you feel about her."

"That is true. Receiving a letter from her makes me very anxious, even before I open it."

"Also, you have carried for many years a great resentment toward your brother for what happened in the death of your son. You have not wanted to face how furious you were with him and how you blamed him, in part, for that tragedy. Nice people do not have such feelings, or so you have always believed."

"I certainly have believed that," she agreed. "It was what had crippled me when I came to see you. What a terrifying way to feel, always fearful that you will be struck down by something you cannot see and cannot understand. I would feel constricting bands around my head—my chest felt as though I were in a vice. The terror would increase as I became afraid once again that I had a brain tumor which had not been discovered."

"How is it now?" I wondered.

"Very different. There are lots of problems, but I know what they are. Facing the feelings of which I was so terribly ashamed has been the most difficult thing I have done, but it has taken an enormous weight off my shoulders. I guess I must face the fact that I will not be a nicer person after therapy."

"You may not be nicer. You will certainly be more real."

When feelings are not acknowledged or confronted they keep the person from maturing in a normal way emotionally. In spite of being a caring and responsible person, Phyllis was operating internally, emotionally, at a great disadvantage. As long as there remained large areas of feeling that she had to avoid she could not mature—she was an emotional child in adult's clothing. Once she was able to face up to, and know her feelings she became not only more comfortable but, as I told her, more real, more authentic, more herself.

To find the true person behind the facade is not always easy. While on the surface two patients may appear quite similar, in fact they may be very different. One patient appears arrogant and conceited, but is really shy, uncertain, and lacking in confidence. His distancing of himself from others represents an attempt to protect himself from the pain he feels in his unfair comparison of himself with others. Another patient gives a similar appearance, but working with his feelings reveals that he is indeed arrogant, has been spoiled into thinking that he is very special and deserves whatever he desires. The sorting out of feelings in the treatment requires a clear understanding of these two very different situations.

It is remarkable how rich is the emotional life of people. To understand ourselves we need to understand a broad array of emotions, some simple, some complex, some subtle, some bold. Some are positive, others are negative, all are important. The most simple emotions stem from the human being's instinctive wish to survive and to propagate the species. From his basic need for food and shelter to sustain and protect him arise concerns about his continued survival—he feels he must acquire and own possessions in order to secure his future. This in turn leads him to compare himself to others and to experience feelings of dissatisfaction, envy, and greed, to name but a few. Other emotions are aroused by his need to ensure the survival of the human race. He wishes to attach and to belong to others, he has feelings of love, sexual attraction, generosity, and on the highest level, trust. He may also have negative feelings of jealousy, mistrust, or even paranoia. Closely connected to all of the feelings of wishing and needing to attach to others are those opposite feelings of pleasure that come from independence, autonomy, self-development, and individuation. When we attach, and when we lose or fear that we may lose those people or those possessions to whom and to which we are attached, we suffer from those feelings of loss which are so debilitating: sadness, depression, loneliness, emptiness, and finally, hopelessness. When we are thwarted in our wish to have what we seek or feel that we need, negative feelings are aroused—anger, rage, destructiveness, murderous or suicidal impulses.

There are numerous other feelings in addition to those that I have mentioned thus far. It is essential that they are explored in therapy if the patient's character is to be understood by himself and the therapist. These include guilt, pride, humility, curiosity, suspicion, and ambition. As well a person may feel grateful or ungrateful, resentful, self-confident, or inferior. Some people have a sense of entitlement which may or may not be justified. Some, but not all, begrudge the good fortune of others. There are sensitive people who feel remorse and regret when they are wrong and there are those who do not care. Happiness, sadness, optimism, pessimism, the list is endless— a vast reservoir of feelings, attitudes, and emotional and mental postures that demand constant attention in the therapeutic situation. Becoming aware of them, sorting them out, and learning to live with them is work that is central to all effective psychotherapy.

DEALING WITH FEELINGS IN THE THERAPY

The feelings within the patient which weave the rich fabric of his personality stem from two sources. Firstly, they spring out of the genetic endowment of that person and are a reflection of the strengths of his natural drives—differences in strength of temperamental drives are evident even in newborns. Secondly, the lifetime experiences of the patient—both good and bad experiences—temper or magnify those innate drives. The task of discovering and revealing as much as possible of this rich fabric is at the heart of psychotherapy. Both therapist and patient must lend themselves to this task. The patient attempts to be as candid and as open as possible, expressing whatever comes into his mind—what he has thought, felt, done, or dreamed. The therapist helps him by enquiring, suggesting, and, when he feels he is able to, explaining and interpreting. No therapist can know at the outset what it is that is wrong in the patient's emotional life. The well-trained, experienced, and sensitive therapist will be in a better position to make reasonable guesses about what is going on than will the therapist who does not have those advantages. In the end, however, the proof lies within the patient who, as the months of therapy proceed, will become more and more adept at recognizing when something is correct or incorrect in regard to his feelings. The wise therapist, armed with not only his common sense but his experience, will know what themes are most common in the hearts of human beings: but he will avoid casting his patients in one common mold, and will, rather, want gradually to learn what are the emotions and what are the problems of any particular patient.

The feelings that the patient brings forward must be considered in two contexts, each of which is very important. The first is the context of the patient's life out in his world. He will talk about feelings toward those with whom he lives and has lived, and those with whom he works and has worked. The second is the context of the relationship between himself and the therapist, for herein will be reflected almost all that takes place between the patient and the important other people in his life. This second context offers a great advantage to the therapist, since the feelings in question arise within a relationship of which he is a living part. He experiences with the greatest immediacy how the patient is with others—both his strengths and his problems—and is therefore in a much better position to learn something real and vital about the patient as a person. I will return shortly to this second and most important context, for it is within it that there arise those distortions which we call transference and countertransference, which offer therapist and patient the opportunity to do the most significant work which can occur in psychotherapy.

I have said that the patient's task is to reveal what he feels, as far as he is able, and that the therapist's first task is to help make that possible. How can one do this? How and why would one expose to another person that of which one is most afraid, embarrassed, and ashamed? One can only do so under the protective umbrella of a relationship of great trust. The more a person has felt the need to keep something entirely to himself, or has felt it to be so private and hurtful that he has been unable to share it even with himself, that is his conscious self, the more trust is required to reveal it, and the more is to be gained by getting it out.

The first task then for the therapist is to create an atmosphere of trust in which painful feelings can be recognized and expressed by the patient. Hidden and unexpressed and unrecognized feelings of all kinds can cause symptoms in the patient, so that the expression and recognition of them will in itself be the first step in providing more comfort for the patient. In the course of uncovering such feelings, because of the threat which they represent to the patient, transient symptoms may also arise. The term *psychosomatic* is used when physical pain is caused by emotional stress. There are some who believe this to mean that such pain is a figment of the imagination—how often we hear "it is all in his head." In fact it is as real as any pain suffered by people whose symptoms have an organic basis.

Barbara wrote to me in this connection as follows:

"There are incredible symptoms which profound feelings can create, especially when unrecognized. For example, I remember my deep-seated chest pains, often in the middle of a session. You would try to get me to relax, but all along it was hard for me to accept that my feelings could cause such intense pain—that it did not stem from something physical. Finally Dr. Brown [the consultant internist] convinced me. Also, there was my recent crippling headache which came because it was the first time I was really hurt by you. For weeks I was terrified I would lose you if I told you that I thought you had been unfair. I realize now that the consequence of criticizing my mother was the removal of her affection and approval and I was afraid you might react in the same way—I should have known better."

In each instance these physical symptoms were severe and disabling, and arose from the threat posed by unrecognized feelings. In each case the symptoms cleared away as soon as the feelings were identified.

It is important to note that what I have been describing as the way in which feelings are handled in therapy is equally important elsewhere in life. Psychotherapy is unique in that it offers the planned opportunity for a safe context in which upsetting feelings can be examined. There are other contexts in which such examination can be of great value. Any human relationship in which intense feelings exist can benefit from candid, courageous confrontation of intense and disturbing feelings. Friendship or marriage can benefit enormously if the partners can, at times, engage in such honest exploration. If, in a parent–child relationship, such open recognition and expression of feelings can occur as the child matures, a closeness will develop between the people concerned which can come about in no other way. True intimacy depends upon revelation of significant feelings between people, whatever the basic nature of their relationship. However, talking about living and talking about feelings is not the equivalent of living and feeling. The quality of life can be significantly augmented by the intimate sharing of feelings, but such discussion and such sharing must not be expected to serve as a substitute for living and feeling. In the same way, psychotherapy can only serve as a way of improving the quality of life, never as a substitute for real life.

People are filled with feelings. Of some of them they are proud, of others ashamed; of some they are aware, of others they are not. The more of these feelings of which they become aware, the stronger will they become and the more comfort, freedom, and control will they have in their lives. Psychotherapy aims to have the patient become aware of the realities of his life, both the outer reality of the world in which he lives and the inner reality—his feelings. Both therapist and patient put their minds to the task of exploring that inner reality. One part of the patient's mind is an observer who joins with the therapist, another observer, in the exploration. Another part of the patient's mind reaches some understanding or insight about the feelings and the behavior which have been observed and experienced. This understanding takes place within the cognitive or thinking or intellectual part of the patient's mind, and is like any other process of self-education, in which someone observes then learns from what he has observed. There is another way in which the patient learns about his feelings, a way which does not use his cognitive apparatus but rather uses his emotional apparatus. In this case the patient learns about his feelings by having, that is experiencing them. It is one thing to say: "Oh yes, I see that I felt jealous of you," and it is quite another to feel inside the impact of intense jealousy. It is one thing to say "I feel quite dependent on her," and quite another to feel the terror of a feared separation from that person. It is one thing to say: "I understand now how disloyal he has been to me," and quite another to feel the rage, humiliation, and defeat which is a spontaneous response to such disloyalty. From such feelings can come "emotional insight," which is not only an understanding of ideas within the mind, but the result of having been through and experienced certain feelings while at the same time examining and understanding them.

The Most Important Context of Feelings in Therapy

I have indicated earlier that feelings examined in the therapy exist in two contexts: of these the feelings that arise within the therapeutic relationship are most important.

The therapist and patient are two real people who come together repeatedly, and so a *real relationship* exists between them. As in any such relationship its qualities derive from the characters and endowments of the two participants, as well as from the particular chemistry of the combination of the two of them. The patient and therapist come together for a purpose, that is, to do some work, so that a *working alliance* is set up between them. Its qualities will also be based upon their two characters—their ability and willingness to work at something, their diligence, their intelligence, sensitivity, and insightfulness. What happens between them will also be markedly affected by the emotional problems which each of them brings to the relationship: it should be the case, since the therapist is trained and experienced and since the patient comes in need of help, that the larger part of such emotional or neurotic distortions in their relationship arise from the patient. Such distortions on the patient's part are called *transference*. Those which arise out of the problems of the therapist are called *countertransference*. When a patient has a surprising and excessive reaction of rage to a relatively minor provocation on the part of the therapist, that is a manifestation of transference. When a patient feels so attached to the therapist that he is overwhelmed with depressive feelings as a vacation approaches, that, too, is transference. When a therapist has a headache preceding each hour of one of his patients, he must recognize his reluctance to meet with the patient, and that is an evidence of countertransference. When either transference or countertransference involves feelings such as love, affection, attraction, or enticement, it is called *positive*. When it involves feelings such as hate, anger, fear, or apprehension, it is called *negative*.

Transference and countertransference are to be expected within any therapeutic relationship. They are neither good nor bad, they are simply a natural result of the fact that two people meet regularly, work hard toward a common purpose, discuss the most intimate of feelings and recollections, and hence become attached in a particularly intensive way. All feelings on the part of the patient are magnified in his dealings with this person who, once a stranger serving a professional function for him, becomes at least for a time one of the most important people in his life.

When Phyllis had a terrible headache because she was so angry with me for my incorrect interpretation about her sister (chapter 8), and that headache disappeared as she dropped a letter to me into the mailbox, that had to do with transference. When Helen raged at me because the help I was giving her was not enough to meet her demands, that too had to do with transference (chapter 8). Margaret's analyst clearly had countertransference feelings when he said, "Do you have to?" on learning that she was planning to leave the analysis (chapter 7).

Strong reactions, such as those of Phyllis and Helen, can serve as most important opportunities to do useful work within the therapy. In each instance the therapist needs to point to what has been happening, show the patient how the strength of her feelings cannot be explained solely by the situation, then seek with the patient the reasons for the strength of the feelings involved. There is no more helpful or instructive step that can be taken in therapy than to focus careful attention on what transpires between patient and therapist and find whatever explanation can be found for the feelings concerned, especially when those feelings are particularly strong.

"There is something from yesterday that I want to discuss with you," I said.

"What is that?" asked Clara.

"You were sarcastic with me."

"I was?" She was surprised. "What did I say?"

"You said that what I had told you about your children was not something that I would apply to myself in my own life."

"Did I? I guess I did. But I didn't think I was being sarcastic."

"You were. Something was bothering you."

"Well, something was. You really hurt me the day before by being offhand. When the end of the hour came I felt that I was rushed out of here. I didn't have time to say what I needed to say."

"How did that make you feel?"

"Terrible. I was so upset I was up most of the night. I was going to write and say I would not come back, but I guess by now I know enough not to do that."

"You felt I was not really interested in you?"

"That's right. It's terrible what an effect that has upon me. I felt all alone and hopeless—and that's when the desperate feelings come."

"The way you felt when left alone as a child?"

"Yes. Alone and hopeless."

We talked about it some more: how her anger had come from feeling hurt by me; how her sarcasm was inappropriate and unwarranted; how she must learn not to deny what she does, but must see it and take responsibility for it. Then it was the end of our time.

"How are you feeling now?" I asked.

She hesitated. "A little better."

"A little?"

"I'm all right now," she said with a smile, despite herself. "I'll see you tomorrow."

The learning about feelings which occurs does not take place at one time, because of the reluctance on the patient's part to learn about uncomfortable truths. Rather, the same lessons are repeated again and again, and have their impact through the patient's finally realizing how he repeatedly hurts himself by the same errors, the same misunderstandings, or the same attitudes. The patient finally sees, especially as it is repeated within the context of his relationship with the therapist, the pattern of self-defeat which he has woven for himself. It is only with such realization that possible better alternative paths become visible.

Edna's first analysis had been deficient in some important ways. There are many aspects of how she had always functioned that had not been made clear to her. We discussed those problems again and again as they arose within our relationship, in her second analysis.

"I don't understand why you became so angry with me yesterday," Edna said.

"Because you are so mistrustful of me, after all this time," I replied. "How could that not affect me?"

"How did I show it?"

"You took offense when I pointed out what you had done that was

wrong. Then you began to be critical of me, and to remind me of how I am never satisfied with the way you are. Then you let me know how I favored the patient who came before you by giving her a few minutes more—despite the fact that I have often, when necessary, done the same for you."

"That is true, I can see that. I try so hard not to attack you, because I really do appreciate that you want to help me. Despite myself I end up doing it again."

"You take offense so easily. You are always ready to feel that you have been slighted. You do that with me and you do it with most other people."

"But I don't do it with Alice and Beth who are my best friends. And I don't think I did it very much with my first analyst."

"You don't do it with Alice and Beth because you feel at some advantage with them. You are better off than they are, and they look up to you and appreciate you for always helping them with their problems. You did it much less with your first analyst because he did not challenge the way you were. He let you feel that you were loved and he accepted your behavior, as a result you were not threatened by him and did not try to change. When I point out your problems you are insulted and take offense."

"That is a very difficult spot I put you in."

"You are right about that—and you do it again and again. It is one of the most important immaturities you still exhibit, and will stand in the way of a relationship with anyone who dares to be fully honest with you."

"Is that the only time it occurs?"

"No. You must watch yourself with most people, and you will see it lurking in the shadows; you are ready to be insulted, ready to be hurt. What comes to the forefront with me is there more subtly with most people."

It required a great many confrontations of this attitude before Edna accepted the validity of what I was pointing out. I had used material from what she had told me about many people, but the most instructive material was that which was drawn from what *happened between the two of us. That had an immediacy which was the most convincing, and finally broke past the denial she had always exercised as to how she really functioned with other people.*

The feelings which arise in the patient are a product of his genetic endowment at birth, his life experiences, and the basic values and attitudes of his character. The exploratory work of the therapy results in the emergence of deeply buried feelings, some of which are startling and unexpected. How a patient copes with such revelations also depends upon his character. The person who has basic humility and sensitivity and is honest enough to face the often painful task of learning about himself will gain the most from treatment.

It is necessary, therefore, for the therapist to explore the roots in character which serve so strongly to produce feelings which would not otherwise be comprehensible. The exploration of such roots moves the therapy from a superficial understanding of feelings alone, to a deeper understanding of the spiritual and creative aspects of the patient.

10

LOVE'S LABOR LOST
Failures in Psychotherapy

THERE are many reasons why psychotherapy can fail. They may reside in the therapist, in the patient, or in the combination of the two of them.

At times the result of therapy is seen by some as being partially successful and by others as a total failure. Take the case of a patient who has been in and out of the hospital with recurrent psychotic episodes. If some years of therapy allow that patient to stay out of the hospital, then the therapist may justifiably feel that he has achieved some measure of success. The patient, on the other hand, might be terribly disappointed that his life is still so limited, and the patient's family, facing the prospect of living with a chronically emotionally disabled person, might see the therapist as having failed in his task.

In some instances it is the therapist and patient who agree that the latter is much improved and those close to him who hold the opposite opinion.

Arthur had always been quiet and acquiescent. Most people who knew him thought well of him, and at the same time felt sorry for him. He flushed easily when embarrassed, and was frequently apologetic, tending to blame himself if anything went wrong in his contacts with others. At work, if an error was made in dealing with a customer or a colleague, he always felt the fault to be his. When friendship failed, he sought for the problem only in himself, not in the friend.

During the course of psychoanalysis Arthur's way of presenting himself to other people changed markedly. He was no longer concerned with their welfare because his own became so important to him. Whereas in the past he had blamed himself if problems arose, he now tended to find fault with those around him. His friends felt glad that he was no longer so easily embarrassed or humiliated. But they missed that modesty which had characterized him, and found him less attractive to be with. He changed his friendships and his loyalties.

Arthur was very pleased with the results of his treatment. Certainly he was more sure of himself, and in less pain. However, the majority of his former friends felt that, even taking into account his undeniable progress, too much that was worthwhile had been sacrificed in the process of treatment.

In this case, the fact that most of the people who know Arthur feel that he has been diminished, makes us wonder whether he and this therapist share a faulty view of Arthur's world. He has been allowed to become too selfish. The therapist should have recognized in the beginning of the treatment that a false modesty covered a true selfishness, and should have challenged that selfishness, rather than encouraged it.

There are other situations, much more numerous, in which most people feel the therapy has had good results but the few people closest to the patient are dissatisfied. This is because they have a false idea of what is best for the patient. For example, a parent who is threatened by the loss of an exceedingly close relationship with a child who is too old for that degree of closeness, will fight to retain that symbiotic connection. In many instances, with patience and perseverance, such an arrangement can be interrupted slowly and gradually, so that both parties have a chance to make the necessary adjustments. When this is not possible the child goes on to lead a separate life, the parent remains resentful and unforgiving, and sees the therapy as having failed.

Excessive seriousness may also cause the therapy to be unsuccessful.

Ralph decided as an adolescent that he would like to be a psychoanalyst. He was an ordinary young man with a light-hearted and pleasant manner who did not take life very seriously. He was an accommodating person, almost to a fault.

Ralph was an average student so it required very hard work and persistence for him to gain admission to medical school. He graduated in the middle of his class, having enjoyed the study of medicine, surgery, obstetrics, and gynecology, but at no point did he seriously consider changing his original goal. He entered a good university residency program to train in psychiatry, and graduated, having done satisfactory but undistinguished work. During his training, he undertook a personal psychoanalysis and was then accepted as a candidate for training in psychoanalysis. During the third and fourth year of his residency a subtle change in him became apparent. In any discussion about psychiatry and psychoanalysis he made it clear that he considered the real and total truth was to be found only in psychoanalytic work, and that psychotherapy performed by psychiatrists was a very great compromise. More important than that, his general demeanor gradually and increasingly changed. He became much less spontaneous. When a question was addressed to him he would pause, muse, and respond minimally if at all. He seemed increasingly to live and think and move with excessive care. He laughed rarely if ever, and had no sense of humor about any aspect of his work.

Shortly before his training as a psychiatrist was to end, I talked with Ralph about his plans.

"What are you expecting to do next year, Ralph?" I asked.

"I plan to do full-time practice."

"Have you considered doing any hospital or agency work with part of your time?"

"I did consider it, but decided against it."

"Why?" I wondered.

"What is done in hospitals and agencies is a waste of time. People are pasted together without facing their real problems. There is only one real treatment, and that is psychoanalysis, so that is what I intend to do."

"Are you saying that all other approaches to which you have been exposed have no use?"

"That's right, that is what I feel."

Ralph remained warm hearted and well intentioned. But he had lost the spontaneity which had been one of his most attractive traits. His manner seemed to say: "Life is very serious, and I will not be drawn into its frivolous mainstream. It is my duty to be calm, unruffled, and analytic, devoted constantly, whether in my consulting room or in my life to the serious business of a psychoanalyst. No other attitude would befit my calling."

There are various ways in which we could respond to the changes in Ralph. I suspect that his analyst considered that this was an excellent result; that before his treatment, the patient had been over-solicitous, too anxious to please, and unreflective, and that this analysis had helped him past these characterological deficiencies. I would say that something most important had gone out of Ralph's life. He had become deadly serious and, in the process, lost much of his natural zestfulness. He illustrates the worst outcome of the application of psychoanalysis as a religion. He has lost his awareness of his limitations and is in his own mind a person of great value, even eminence. It is true, of course, that it is important to work on improving a patient's self-image but only if the final result is the emergence of his true character. Ralph works long hours as a dedi-

cated psychoanalyst. He will continue to do much good work. Some of his patients will benefit from his dedication. Those who, like himself, take all that their analyst says and does as best and right, will end up much as he has. Many will, either during or following their treatments see that much of life is missed by such an attitude, and will grow beyond the model he provides for them. When middle age comes and passes, Ralph himself is in significant danger of feeling that he has wasted the best part of himself, that is, the emotional part. Then he will have to make some major changes if he is able to do so and it is not too late.

There is one form of failure about which there is rarely any disagreement, and that is suicide. Death is the ultimate opponent to whom the physician may lose the patient. When the psychotherapist is a psychiatrist, then that part of him which is a physician must, as do all physicians, be concerned with the physical health and the life of the patient. That life can be threatened in several ways. The medical therapist must listen carefully for any indication of physical illness and arrange, either through his own efforts or by referral to a colleague, to diagnose and treat such illness. The nonmedical therapist must be certain that a physician assumes these responsibilities with the patient. All therapists must judge whether the patient or any other person is in danger because of the patient's emotional problems.

A patient may be so disturbed as to make choices which are against his best interests. For example, if he is elated he may suddenly spend all his money unwisely or contract unrealistic debts. I know of one patient who, in a fit of excessive self-confidence, bought three houses he could not afford. Or a patient may, through lack of ability to make sensible judgments put himself in a dangerous position, by agreeing to engage in an illegal adventure. Some patients cannot see that they are in physical danger at the hands of someone else; for example, a wife who refuses to leave her husband who is repeatedly threatening her. Conversely there are those who are so disturbed that they may be a danger to others through homicide, or to themselves through suicide. It is the therapist's task to evaluate such dangers, and, if necessary, take measures to prevent them. Usually the first measure is to share one's concern with the patient. In most instances, if the therapy is being successful, this will suffice, and the danger will be averted. But sometimes, if the therapist's influence is insufficient or the patient too disturbed, it does not suffice, and the danger may remain. This will then place an additional burden upon the therapist who requires, as a member of society, to be concerned not only with the patient's well-being, but also with that of others. And so, at times, the patient will have to be admitted to a hospital to protect himself or others who may be in danger.

Every therapist has, in time, some experience with the suicide of a patient. This is always a painful experience. The following was my first contact with a successful suicide.

The incident occurred when I was chief resident in psychiatry, during the final year of my training. A middle-aged woman, who had been depressed on several occasions over a period of ten years, was on the private psychiatric service. I never saw her, as she was under the care of the chief of the department. But nominally she was, as were all the patients in the department of psychiatry, my responsibility. One afternoon she was discovered by the nurses on the ward, having drowned herself in the bathtub.

It was my task to review what had allowed this to happen. I felt very troubled by the event, and made administrative arrangements which would make a recurrence even less possible than under the previous arrangements: this involved more careful checking and observation of such patients when using the bath facilities. Although she was not under my direct care, I struggled with the terrible sense of loss and waste and the responsibility which all of the staff of the hospital shared.

The next such experience, which took place about eight years later, hit much closer to home.

Robert was thirty-two years of age, single, and worked in a cleri-cal job for a large firm. He came for treatment because he would sometimes become depressed, and because his life felt so unsatisfac-tory to him. He regretted that he was not married. After high school he had gone directly to his current place of work. He had only a few friends. He lived in an apartment by himself, and saw his parents every few weeks.

I suggested that we meet once a week in psychotherapy. He agreed. After about a year of regular visits, he seemed moderately improved. He did not complain of as much depression. He saw the possibilities of more friendships, and more happiness in the future. Or so he said.

Three days after I had last seen him, a session which in no way had aroused my concern, I received a phone call from his family physician. Robert had been discovered in his apartment, having died of an overdose of sleeping medication which he had bought over the counter, at a drugstore. This was a shocking experience for me. Even in retrospect I could not account for his suicide, and I tried very hard to do so. I felt very upset about this outcome. In a most striking way, therapy had failed. Robert had clearly had feelings which he had not been prepared to share with me—probably includ-ing hopelessness and a deep sense of failure.

Although it is not typical, I choose this example because it was a profound experience. In most cases a successful suicide is not a complete surprise to the therapist because there has been some evidence that it might occur. The vast majority of people who are in danger of committing suicide can be helped not to do so. It is hopelessness which makes one want to die.

As I have stressed, the resurrection of hope is a chief aim of psychotherapy. In most instances, as hope returns, the danger of suicide diminishes.

In regard to the potential for suicide in his patient, the therapist faces a serious, but not surprising dilemma. It is the same dilemma that confronts the parent. The parent wishes to protect the child from harm. If he is too free and careless with his child, the child may be hurt, whether by fire, or by falling, or by passing automobiles. But if the parent is so concerned that he overprotects the child, the child will grow up either phobic or foolish, and in either event, unprepared to look after himself. Similarly, the therapist must not allow the patient's life to be in danger. However, if he is too careful, the patient will not grow to be able to handle his own life, and to protect himself. When the patient is a severe suicidal risk, the therapist's decisions, as a result, are often very difficult to make. The experienced therapist of sound judgment will make few errors, but if he were never to err he would have to exercise too great a degree of caution which would, in the end, be crippling for his patients.

An entirely different reason for failure, residing within the patient, may exist. The following is an example:

When I had been in practice about five years, a man was referred for treatment by his family physician. Richard was thirty-eight, well-dressed, and rather short in stature. He was clearly intelligent, and very well spoken. During his first visit he told me that he was depressed because, after very great financial successes, he had run into business reverses. He had worked for newspapers, and in the printing business, and had done varied promotional work. He told of his rapid rise in the business world and characterized himself as very popular with friends and colleagues.

At the end of the consultation I suggested that psychotherapy might be of help, twice a week. He was a well-endowed person who,

I told him, could likely discover the things which he was doing which were to his disadvantage. These had not only led to his reverses at work, but threatened to bring such further difficulties in the future. I felt that he would be well advised to do some work on these character traits before they caused him more problems.

Richard agreed to my suggestion. The first two occasions he came on time, and continued his easy-going talk about himself. The third time he was quite late, but had a plausible explanation. The next several times he was either late or missed the appointment. No effort to have him accept any responsibility for what took place was of any avail. Suddenly he stopped coming. Two months later he called and asked for an appointment. I wondered why he had stopped earlier without saying he would do so. He offered elaborate explanations of unavoidable external problems. I said I would see him once more to discuss what had happened. He didn't keep the appointment. Nor did he pay for any of his visits to me. I did not hear from him again.

Richard had no interest in changing. Though I wondered during the original visit whether this might be the case, I was not at all sure. He had come to a psychiatrist with the vague notion that such a person might be of use to him. He was in the habit of putting people to some use. He saw all difficulties as residing in the other person, or in the situation around him, but never in himself. He knew when he was uncomfortable, he preferred not to be so, and if he could, he would manipulate those around him to remove the discomfort from himself. He was not affected by anyone else's discomfort and like Rachael (in chapter 7) felt entirely justified in making things as right for himself as he possibly could.

It didn't take long for him to understand that psychotherapy would not be of any use to him. He wanted to get out of the uncomfortable place in which he found himself, but doing so did not include the possibility of his making any changes within himself. We did not speak the same language, and we did not see the world in the same way. He was quick to understand this. I was slower. Because of this irresolvable difference, psychotherapy failed.

Richard presents a rather stark example of someone who cares little for others and is not the least disturbed by their concerns or their discomforts. I do not know the proportion of such people in the population. Most of them would not be seen by a psychotherapist, as they would not see therapy as either desirable or useful.

Most of us fall into intermediate categories wherein we put ourselves and our own needs first, yet we can still feel some real concern about the welfare of others. Some such people, when they are disturbed, behave as though they do not care, when in fact they care very much. Here there is an extremely important distinction to be made. With disturbed adolescents, for example, it is all too easy to be taken in by the bravado and "coolness" of the patient. Beneath a pose of unconcerned condescension may be a state of keen concern for what others think or do. The therapist will have to make this distinction. When there is doubt, it is better for the therapist to err on the side of excessive trust, rather than on the side of excessive suspiciousness. When caring lies behind manifest unconcern, the patient can, once he has learned to trust the therapist, be reached, and be helped to change. When the opposite is the case, the patient will not be reached, and no change will ensue.

There are other instances in which therapy does not succeed where no such striking reasons exist as those in the illustrations above. Sometimes it is simply that the combination of the two people does not work.

Geraldine was a psychologist who had been in treatment with two different psychiatrists before she had started her professional training. Both had helped her to a moderate degree, but in each case she felt she had grown beyond them, and wanted more intensive treat-ment. She was referred to me for psychoanalysis. I agreed that she could expect some further help from analysis, for she was intelli-gent, hard working, and had a driving ambition to further improve her life and her way of functioning.

I saw Geraldine for about a year and a half. The course of our work was pressured and stormy. On the one hand, we did make some beginning at understanding the origins of the difficulties which she had with others. She was clever and energetic, she was easily hurt, and she was frustrated. On the other hand, from the beginning of the analysis she felt a strong dissatisfaction with the treatment, and with me. She had a marked tendency to idealize the analyst, and an equal or stronger tendency to disparage him. We worked on this a great deal. But always she was left with the feeling that something essential was missing from the therapeutic relationship.

"I came to you because I thought you could accomplish something the others couldn't—because I felt that full psychoanalysis was the only method that could help me," she said.

"That is what you felt," I agreed.

"But something is wrong with how you deal with me," she com-plained. "You are not doing your best."

"You want me to be very strong and able. Yet you insist that I do things your way."

"Your explanations must be too simple. Somehow we don't go into things deeply. I have a strong idea of how analysis should be, and it doesn't feel that way. The things you tell me don't help."

"They not only don't help you, they don't feel at all good to you. You seem fixed in the attitude that what I am doing for you is wrong," I replied.

"I was certain that you could help me, but something is missing."

In the end, for these reasons, the treatment failed. The analysis was interrupted for a time because of my being ill. This break led, with my agreement, to her consulting other analysts and, finally, to her changing to another analyst.

Geraldine and I met at a professional meeting after her new analysis had been underway about a year. We were pleased to see one another, but a slight sense of awkwardness existed. She said that her analysis was proceeding slowly, but with apparent success. She said that despite the fact that she had stopped her work with me, she felt nonetheless that some valuable things had come out of it. Both of us knew that we had tried very hard, but could not succeed. Something had been missing from the combination of the two of us.

Geraldine had developed a mistrust of me that would not go away, and in the end the analysis foundered upon it. Several years later she called and asked to see me. She was just completing her analysis. She felt that it had helped her in many ways, though not as much as she had expected. In retrospect she found that much of what we had done together had been of importance to her, and she regretted that her feelings had made it impossible for us to carry the work further—but they had made it impossible, and this was something that, in looking back over the years, we both had to accept.

Of the several types of failures I have listed, the most disturbing, of course, is that which ends in suicide. The next most upsetting, I believe, is that in which, despite long, sustained effort on the parts of both patient and therapist, the results are severely disappointing.

Helen, whose problems I have discussed at length, and with whom I had much difficulty, was treated over a period of many years. In the course of treatment she did change considerably, so that she was able to broaden her base of social and vocational activities, but she continued to have depressive periods. A large variety of medication was tried, but none gave her sustained help. In the end she found it best to use no medication at all.

Her psychotherapy was to terminate, and she was terribly disappointed with the results.

"You told me I would get better," Helen cried, on the last occasion when we met.

"That is true, I said you would improve, and you have, in many ways," I replied. "It is also true that you are not as well as both of us would prefer."

"You have to find a way to make me better. I cannot accept how upset I can still become."

"It isn't that I have to. It seems I cannot."

"But how can I live with that?" she asked.

"You are not through changing," I answered. "I do not really know how much further you can get. All I do know is that we have gone as far as we can together. For you to see me any longer only inflames you because I cannot do more. You now have to see what happens on your own."

"You put a lot into it, I admit," she said, "but I put in even more. It is my life, not yours, which is so unacceptable."

'I agree. But there is nothing more I can do about it."

Helen consulted with other psychiatrists. They made a variety of suggestions, none of which she felt to be helpful. One of them told her that she would be best advised to have no more treatment, and to take a fuller responsibility for her own life. That opinion, too, had been unsatisfying.

Time will tell how much further she will go. In such an instance it seemed necessary to point out that she was wrong to assume that there was more that the therapist could achieve. Both patient and therapist could conclude that they had accomplished a good deal. But both of us admitted that the end result was a severe disappointment.

Our final meeting was sad and frustrating. We each had to accept that we had gone as far as we were able to go together; and that it was not far enough.

To be a psychotherapist, one must not give up easily. At times, in all intensive treatment, the participants feel that further progress is impossible. To give up the treatment too readily is a serious mistake. The capacity to persevere beyond exhausting and discouraging times is one of the cardinal requisite qualities of an effective therapist. But sometimes one should give up.

All patients have a right to try to find a therapist who suits them. If, in a therapist's mind, it is always the fault of the patient when therapy does not succeed, then that therapist is unfair and unduly unaware of his limitations. When the combination does not work, the therapist must be prepared to have the patient work instead with a colleague. This is in keeping with a very old tradition in medicine: both patient and doctor have the freedom to accept or reject the idea of working together. The principle holds true in all psychotherapy, equally so when the therapist is from a discipline other than medicine.

While discussing failures, it is important to consider an area which is related, and yet is very different: mistakes. Everyone, including all psychotherapists, makes mistakes. Some are important, and some are not. When the therapist makes an error in explaining what he believes lies behind a certain problem in the patient, that is a mistake, but one with which, under the right circumstances, the patient will be able to live. When the relationship is not contingent upon the omniscience of the therapist, the patient will simply disagree. The therapist may then ask: "Well, if that doesn't feel right, how do you see it?" And the patient may then be able to modify the miss or near-miss into a more fully correct explanation. When a mistake occurs because the therapist is bored, arrogant, uninterested, or uncaring, the patient will become aware of this and the therapy will fail.

If a therapist forgets an appointment, double books his patients, or does not remember what the patient has told him, this is always important, but the patient will be able to make allowances for these lapses as long as he feels that the therapist is working with integrity and care. The patient needs to discover and accept the natural human limits of the therapist, but he cannot be expected to tolerate mistakes which arise from the therapist's lack of concern for his welfare.

11

LOVE'S LABOR WON
A Good Result in Psychotherapy

ONE of the principal difficulties that psychotherapy faces has been around the question of goals. Often no goals have been formulated, and so one is not clear, in the end, whether or not one has had a good result. On the other hand, too often unrealistic goals have been set which are impossible to attain. Who can resolve the infantile neurosis? No one whom I have met. Who can become free of transference distortions? No patient or therapist whom I have had the pleasure to know. Who can become free of neurosis, fully analysed, or even free of conflicts? To idealize the goals of psychotherapy is to invite failure, for at the end of the most long, intensive, and effective therapy what is left is a human being who still has limits and frailties.

When the expectations of psychotherapy are reasonable, a great deal can be accomplished and the success of the treatment can be measured in several ways. One is that the disturbances which we call symptoms can disappear. Fears or phobias, for example, can diminish or vanish, and anxiety or depression can clear away. Another is that the patient can become more realistically adaptive to his or her life, understanding more clearly what lies within himself and what surrounds him. That understanding will lead to further progress, as the patient becomes more able to accept the limits placed upon him and to take advantage of any opportunities which may arise.

A third way in which improvement can be measured is that the patient may become more able to get close to people and form trusting bonds with a few of them. This can give him a sense of warmth and completeness he cannot achieve in any other way—for people are, in themselves, basically incomplete emotionally. They need to be supplemented by others in order to have a sense of wholeness. Many people have learned to be so untrusting that they cannot and do not form viable, continuous connections. And so they feel incomplete, frustrated, alienated, and empty. A host of acquaintances or even friends brings a limited satisfaction. A deep and trusting relationship with a few people is considerably more fulfilling. Being able to form such close connections is one of the good results of successful treatment.

Another is that the patient may, having become more aware of what is within him, be better able to make use of his innate capacities. Almost all of us use only the very smallest part of our potential: that is true physically, emotionally, and intellectually. A healthy person uses only one-tenth of the cells of his liver. Should he destroy three-quarters of his liver, for example through the cirrhosis which comes from chronic alcohol intake, he will still not enter a state of liver failure. Many people do not become aware of their full capacity to learn, to create, to solve problems, or to develop. Successful therapy allows the patient to recognize more fully what lies unused or undeveloped within him and frees him to make use of what he has found there. Such use may very well be for the good of society, since people in general ordinarily benefit when any of us is more productive. As for the patient, he will discover new opportunities and find an inner satisfaction which is available in no other way. It is easiest to illustrate this by a physical analogy. If I only walk slowly, wherever I go, I will probably always have a sense of torpid lethargy, but if I run or swim every day I will feel stimulated and fresh, and so it is with all of our potentials. We have evolved to use ourselves fully, and when we do so we feel better: this applies to our bodies, our minds, and our emotions. So, if someone learns in therapy that he has a talent for music or for writing and takes steps to develop that gift, he will then feel more fulfilled and creatively alive than he felt before.

A further way in which psychotherapy can help is by freeing the person to take pleasures in responsible ways. Many people are blocked from enjoying themselves, not just because they have not cultivated their innate capacities, but because they feel too guilty to do so. They may have been taught that pleasure is evil, or frivolous, or superficial, or selfish. They may have been encouraged to suffer and repent, rather than to enjoy or relish or cherish or celebrate. The roots of such attitudes, which originate in the family or subculture, may be discovered during the process of psychotherapy. Once recognized, the patient can change and become freer to enjoy his life. I use the word responsible because, if that which is pleasurable is taken by sacrificing the feelings of others, then the cost is too high for all concerned. The patient will, if he is successful in therapy, be aware of whether or not he exploits people or ignores their welfare. And he will learn to find enjoyment which is not at the expense of others and might even, if he is fortunate, be to their advantage.

When Jane was very ill in the hospital the important question was how she would again be able to live a life on the outside. When she began to improve, one of the activities she enjoyed was the program in ceramics. She soon showed that she had a considerable untapped potential in this direction. A year after her discharge from the hospital a number of the staff were invited to the opening of the first showing of her work in ceramics. She was enormously pleased with the success of the show, and with the fact that quite a few of the staff had attended. Jane and I talked for a while and she was excited and grateful to have come so far. All of the guests were circulating to look at the pieces, and before the end of the evening most of this new artist's work had been sold.

I spent considerable time selecting a piece for myself. I found a bowl delicately painted in blue which I arranged to buy. It sits on the windowsill of my office now. Often as I talk with patients I will glance at that bowl and remember Jane and how ill and hopeless she was. I am always encouraged and refreshed with the memory of how much she has accomplished.

What the bowl tells me is not only that she managed to get past her suicidal hopelessness and out into the world. More than that, she discovered areas of herself which were uncharted, capacities which were undeveloped. She had undertaken to exploit those capacities in ways which were satisfying to herself and to others, and this product gives testimony to that fact.

In the bottom of the bowl lies a small card which reads: "Thank you for joining in the celebration. Love, Jane."

Psychotherapy does not in itself create something new. What it does is form an environment in which the patient can begin to explore and to stretch and to unfold and hence to grow. That growth is not stimulated or caused by the psychotherapy. Rather, the therapeutic experience removes some of those impediments and blocks which have stood in the way of natural growth and maturation.

The various ways in which successful psychotherapy can help that I have outlined above are each important and each quite different. During psychotherapy, which occurs over a period of many months or a number of years, each of these will be taking place alongside the others. Often a patient comes into psychotherapy because of manifest symptoms: a severe depression precipitated by a loss, or a psychotic breakdown finally brought on after years of unhappy and frustrated living. Thus the early months of treatment may be marked by the clearing of the symptom in question. The depression or the anxiety may diminish in intensity, decrease in frequency, and then disappear. The delusions (false ideas) or hallucinations (voices or visions) may become less intense and finally cease. The patient has then become much more like others in the general population. Sometimes that is taken to be all that the patient needs to do—that is to "return to his previous personality," or to "come back to a normal homeostatic balance." If the attitude of the therapist is that this is sufficient, the patient may then be discharged from treatment and returned to his normal life.

Such a person, since only a limited change has had time to occur, is at very great risk of falling ill again. For it is insufficient simply to help him return to a state where he is again free of major symptoms. It is most likely that he will break down again, because not enough has been done to eliminate the causes of the original breakdown which brought him into treatment. Such therapy, when it occurs in psychiatric hospitals, or in psychiatric departments of general hospitals, leads to a "revolving door" situation, where patients require repeated admissions because the basic causes of difficulty are not addressed and eradicated.

Economic considerations of course enter into these matters. Because psychotherapy is expensive, since it is time-consuming, and the time of professional workers is costly, short cuts are often sought or demanded. Patients are brought in and out of the hospital, or in and out of office treatment, and their discharge effected as rapidly as possible. This helps chiefs of departments pass on pleasing statistics to the executive directors of their hospitals, who in turn take pride in passing them on to the government agencies or insurance companies who in large part bear the costs of the treatment. The duration of the treatment is thus kept briefer, at least on paper, and that appears to represent a savings to society. In fact, the same individuals are continually returning for further help, and, being unable to be consistently employed, are consuming large amounts of public funds, in the form of welfare or other benefits. This then, is a false saving in the short run, which leads to enormous cost in the long run.

Carrie is easy to remember, because she was the first patient admitted for treatment in a new psychiatric inpatient unit. The staff had met together regularly to plan how the unit would function, and what principles would be followed in their work together. One such principle was that an attempt would be made to give patients enough time in treatment so that they would really improve in a substantial way, and have the base established which would allow them to go forward and hold on to whatever gains had been made.

Carrie was then seventeen years of age. She had been treated in a number of hospitals. She was dependent on several street drugs. She had made numerous attempts to commit suicide, the most recent of which had brought her to the emergency room of this hospital, then to the medical department for treatment, and from there to the psychiatric unit. She was failing in high school, although she appeared to be of excellent intelligence. She was attractive and gifted, but also challenging, rebellious, and iconoclastic. She was bound up in a symbiotic relationship with her mother, who wished that she would grow up but was frightened by any moves her daughter made to separate from her. In turn, the patient was on the one hand scathingly critical of her mother, and on the other hand afraid to leave her.

"How do you feel about being here, Carrie?"

"So-so. I have nothing better to do."

"Do you expect that we can help you?"

"I feel two ways about that. I have failed too often to be optimistic about the result of my stay here. My life is a mess, and I don't see any way of changing that. Still I suppose I must have some hope that something good will happen, or I would not have agreed to come here."

"We'll see what we can do."

Carrie's stay in the hospital was marked by swings up and down. She was depressed, anxious, and suicidal at times, enthusiastic, energetic, and optimistic at others. She worked diligently in psychotherapy for periods, and in between fell into a state of hopeless, sarcastic defeatism. As the months passed she began to talk with her therapist about doing professional work in the future. She temporarily resumed some schoolwork while still in the hospital. She identified with her doctor, a young woman, and began to consider becoming a physician and perhaps a psychiatrist. Much work was done with her and her mother by her doctor and a social worker, trying to make use of the positive bond which existed between them, but at the same time attempting to help them separate enough for both of them to live individual lives.

Carrie stayed in the hospital about eight months during that first admission. She was then discharged and made up courses so that she could begin college. She was later readmitted for a few other briefer stays. In total she spent some months over a year in the hospital.

It was never felt by the staff that the psychotherapy which took place in the hospital could itself be enough to allow Carrie to do the changing and growing which were necessary. Whenever she was out of the hospital she carried on with her therapist, working out what were her needs, what were her problems, what might be her goals.

Carrie completed undergraduate work, then went abroad to study for a master's degree. Seven years after her original admission to the hospital she wrote to a former fellow patient. She wanted the staff to know that she was now considered an expert in her field of study,

and two major universities abroad had urged her to join their staff
and take a Ph.D. degree. She had accepted one offer and was looking
forward to the work there. She wrote in part:

"Can you do me a favor? If you're still going to the hospital, can
you spread the news . . .

"It's weird—during the job interview I realized that I'm now an
'expert' on attitudes and communications. I never thought I'd be an
expert! . . . So now I'm beginning to believe that what happens to
me is a result of myself rather than luck, i.e., I guess I'm accepting
responsibility now.

"Well, I must go now, since it's late. See you soon, say hi to the
kids,

Take care,

Love,

Carrie"

Carrie had not been hurried, for like child rearing and education,
therapy cannot be hurried. There is no way in which a child can be
rushed into being an adult, or a student into being an educated
person. The process of psychotherapy, since its best result includes
character maturation and growth of self-confidence and self-esteem,
requires time in addition to effort. Carrie had to learn in numerous
ways: through what she understood cognitively in the therapy;
through what she felt toward, with, and against her therapist, and
through what she discovered by trial and error in her attempts to
become a separate person from her mother. The psychotherapy was
long and painful, for Carrie had to face the conflict between her
terror at the prospect of separating and her yearning to have a full
and independent life.

The illustration of Carrie is useful for several reasons while
we are considering the question of a good result. The most
striking aspect of what happened to her was that a young
woman, struggling to come out of adolescence into adulthood,

went from a vulnerable and dangerous position to a positive and productive one. She had run the grave risk of being damaged, dead by her own hand, or being a permanent ward of society. Instead she is most likely to become an important contributor not only to her own welfare, and to those close to her, but to society at large. With respect to the many months she spent in a hospital inpatient psychiatric unit, this was necessary and unavoidable, for less than that would have been insufficient to get her off the self-destructive track, turn her around, and help her to head in a positive direction. One continuous period in the hospital would not have been as helpful as several separate periods. For in the end, all of the work could not be done in the hospital, because her life lay outside, and she had to attempt repeatedly to reengage with that real life.

Similarly, not all of the growing up that Carrie had to do could be done while still seeing her doctor in psychotherapy. The changes that were initiated in the treatment would unfold and develop over many years—probably for the rest of her life. Rather than making poor, self-destructive choices, she was now making good, constructive ones each of which helped her to progress.

There is another important point that needs to be made with respect to Carrie, and that has to do with the relative degree of her dependence and her independence. It was clear from the start that one of the larger problems was her need to feel a separate person in her own right, without totally rejecting or even destroying those principal attachments which she had formed as a child. Within the psychotherapeutic relationship this problem would of necessity, have to be dealt with. A patient such as Carrie would have to be very suspicious of her therapist in the beginning. As she came to trust the therapist more, and as she became more confident about herself, she would identify with, lean on, emulate, and take strength from her therapist. This would be, naturally, satisfying and even flattering to the therapist. As I have said before, a truly good result in the therapy can only occur if the therapist wants the patient to grow as much as possible into a separate person. If the overt or covert message of the therapist is: "You are free to grow in order to reflect well on me, who has set you free; and you are free to change only into what I am or what I prefer for you, since I of course know what is best for you," then the patient will not do well, and in the end she will remain the child, now bound to a new mother.

If, on the other hand, the therapist conveys this message: "I will help you because I like to help you; I will get you started but you will have to finish the job, because it is your life and not mine; I will be pleased when you find qualities in me that match your own, and you choose them and they become a natural part of you; I will be equally pleased when what you find in me does not suit you, and you put it aside and choose what you recognize as more appropriate for yourself; I am delighted by your growth and development and although I will miss you, I shall be able to accept with pleasure the time when you will no longer need anything from me." Then the patient, if she hears the message, will do well, since she will feel free to be herself and that is the very best possible result.

A good result cannot be evaluated when the patient and the therapist stop meeting for therapy. This is not only because the changes require many years to develop; it is also because the fuller aspect of the patient's self-reliance can only flower when the patient is on her own.

A good result in psychotherapy means that the patient has become able to be close to others. Independence without the capacity for close loving relationships is one sided and unsatisfying. To achieve this goal the patient will have had to allow

need for
is going
job and
therapy

gs that
, and I
impor-
s, and
d new
why
rson,
n."
, at a
Such
lt in

le therapist, and to feel the full impact
for the therapist. She will also have had
ion that the therapist cares for her. Too
patient is brought to look at her angry,
feelings, but is not required to look at her
elings. When these latter are dealt with
ent comes in time to feel less frightened
ith loving feelings. She realizes that close-
ous, but rewarding and fulfilling, not a
gth. As one patient put it to me: "It is a
were friend and not Freud."

ve dealt with both the problems of attaching
ing separate from them, will end up in the
on: they can attach closely enough to draw
ccor from others, and they can go out into the
at is indicated. Not everyone achieves this goal
extent, but a good result will always have such a
of what the therapy hopes to accomplish.

ent who has had a good result is still someone who
ce needed help, may need help in the future. It is
sirable goal to be able never to see the therapist
patient may do very well for years, and then, under
ss of one of life's more demanding times, need to turn
again to the therapist for help. At a time of becoming
ed, having a child, sustaining the death of a near rela-
the former patient may feel the need for further, proba-
few and brief, meetings with the former therapist. If he
els free to contact the therapist, use some help to get over
the difficult time, then continue on his own again, this will
be a good result. The flexibility to know when one needs
help and to arrange for it at those times, puts the former
patient in a very good position and protects him from serious
future difficulties.

Marie (whom I mentioned in chapter 2 while discussing the
self-awareness in the therapist) wrote to tell me that she w
through a difficult time, having felt obliged to give up her
seek further training. In her letter she looked back upon her
in this way:

"I left the job because I couldn't stomach the nasty thir
were openly being done. You taught me to stand up and figh
am doing just that. I still have my integrity, and that is most
tant. Every time I get really down, I think of our session
eventually I get up and push on. I really do get 'flashbacks' ar
insights from those sessions, and they help me to understand
I'm functioning as I do today . . . You really helped. I'm a p
and not just a shadow, or a puppet, because of your interventio

Marie wrote this almost ten years after the therapy had ended
time when we would see each other once every year or two.
continued growth is an excellent illustration of a good resu
psychotherapy.

12

A SIMPLE HUMAN PROCESS

In the earlier chapters I have described many of my feelings about my work. In this final chapter I would like to speak of the conclusions I have reached at this time. It has taken me twenty-five years of practicing psychotherapy to arrive at this place and I have no doubt I will continue to move and to change and refine my ideas.

"Dear Dr. Greben:

This letter is for your 'happy file.' I sometimes think psychiatrists have it rough because they put in a lot of time and effort with people who eventually move on and they seldom hear what has happened to those people. I want you to know what has happened to me.

"I credit you and me and our 'therapy' for my being where I am today. There are so many things I got out of therapy that are still influencing my life.

"You made me feel that I was important to you. You chose to spend an hour of your time with me week after month after year. You could have spent that time with any number of other people and so I felt special.

"I got from you the message that I was responsible for me and that I couldn't depend on other people for anything—including my emotional satisfaction. I learned that I could be in control of my future—

that to a great extent things just don't 'happen' to us unless we choose to do nothing to direct our lives.

"You gave me a sense of self-worth with its resultant self-confidence. That has helped me through some very difficult days during the past three years. I can remember saying to you one day . . . 'but, I don't do hard things!' Well, you can strike that from my record now—I do indeed do hard things!

"You gave me a feeling of warmth and caring that had a very nurturing effect on me. I haven't forgotten that.

"I learned the fine art of perseverance. Just sticking with therapy through the years was evidence of perseverence itself. It has stood me in good stead as I learned how to cope with the unbelievable mountain of work that befalls students in my course . . .

"As I think about it, it seems that all those things happened because of our relationship. I think that relationship is the key to successful therapy. Because of our relationship, which was strong and reliable and stable I learned how to take risks and I value that highly.

"But all of my learning didn't take place while I was in therapy. Part of my growing took place afterwards. It's a progressive thing which happened and continues to happen slowly over the years, but the seeds for it were sown during our time together.

"I want you to know that I treasure my memories of therapy. It was a very important and worthwhile part of my life. If you knew me today you would say that I have a very positive outlook on life. That comes from a variety of factors in my life but a good part of it comes from my association with you.

"Just in case you are beginning to feel like 'God' from all these compliments, be assured that I didn't see you as perfect. There were some things I thought you didn't do very well. But our relationship was strong enough to withstand the stress of your faults and on balance you are very effective.

"I would love to have a visit with you this summer. Maybe we can plan something after I return to Toronto.

"Thanks for contributing to my happiness. Take care.

Sincerely,
Martha"

For me, the work of psychotherapy is as serious as life itself, since life often depends upon it. A response which is felt as rejecting or cruel to the patient may resurrect the danger of suicide: poor judgment on the part of a therapist may mislead the patient or leave him so vulnerable that his life moves in directions which are destructive to him. It is essential therefore, that society, as well as the therapist, understands the responsibility invested in those who do this work. Patients need to be taken seriously by their therapists, for they will experience many sobering feelings during the course of psychotherapy: sadness, loneliness, terror, shame, and humiliation to name only a few.

I will quote, once again, Hannah Green, the author of *I Never Promised You a Rose Garden*, who ended a speech to a group of psychoanalysts with the following words:

> There are things you can never know unless you have been on both sides of the bars. One is the tremendous distance between sickness and health, another is the incredible value of the work you do, and another is the gratitude that the recovered have for the facts of a normal contact with life.

The practice of psychotherapy is challenging, demanding, and most rewarding. Our understanding of people is always incomplete: what remains to be understood is infinite. All we can do is to keep trying to recognize our ignorance and to clear away our misapprehensions. I was somewhat intimidated when I began doing this work with its many varied facets, for it seemed clear that I could never achieve a sense of true mastery. Yet as the years have passed I have become increasingly confident that, although my results can never be perfect, I am able to practice in a way which benefits most patients to a very significant degree. More and more I have been content to accept this as a worthwhile accomplishment.

I have referred several times to the fact that, in the course of therapy, it is not only the patient who changes but also the therapist. As I have changed over the years I have come to realize that formulas and theories are sadly lacking in what they offer the practitioner: in fact they threaten to lay a dead hand upon the psychotherapy. For example, an entire language has been developed which attempts to describe the various functions or portions of the psyche. Three very good examples are id, ego, and superego. These words have been used as a shorthand to help us to think, write, and converse about how people function. But much of the literature on psychotherapy sounds as though egos and ids really exist. Of course they do not, any more than any other concept or representation really exists. We can talk about honesty, and that helps us understand a quality, but when we begin to sound as though honesty could be measured, or weighed, or even recognized in broad daylight, we have gone too far. The most serious problem that comes from taking theoretical constructs too seriously is that what will be lost is the person. When people hurt or are ill or are underdeveloped in any way, what needs to be treated is not an ego, and not a diagnostic category, but a person. The danger of excessive theoretical orientation is that the treatment process itself will become vapid and dehumanized.

I have seen more and more clearly that psychotherapy is a simple human process between two individuals. As little as possible should stand between them, for the greatest changes will arise out of their confrontation emotionally, and their examination of the intimate aspects of that meeting. Those two people come as *themselves,* not as representatives of the categories of *patient* and *therapist.* Early in my training I was taught, I believe incorrectly, to keep myself as an individual out of the therapy. I now know this to be both impossible and undesirable. Whatever I have achieved has necessitated using those personal idiosyncratic qualities which are so much a part of me: my personality, my character, my values, my attitudes, my prejudices, my hesitations, my ambitions, my goals, my curiosities; all these and many more. No matter what I have been taught, or what I have managed to learn, or how I have been affected by my own analysis, I am undeniably and characteristically still only me, and all that I do in the course of my psychotherapeutic work gives evidence of that.

When I remember what has happened over the years with my patients I do so in a highly personal way. Each relationship had its own special value and unique quality which could never be duplicated. As one struggles in the therapeutic process one feels love and terror, intimacy and outrage, concern and humiliation. The patient learns in many ways to trust the therapist and in turn the therapist learns to trust him. There is nothing mysterious about such an experience; it is the heart of psychotherapy but it also happens elsewhere in life. When it does, people can change irreversibly. It is one of life's most profound experiences, one in which risks are taken and a person can learn to expose himself and admit that he needs and depends upon another. When he can successfully engage in a trusting and intimate relationship he will grow and become a more integrated person.

This unique and individual quality of the therapy can be influenced in certain ways. One is when psychotherapy becomes less art and science and more religion. For the patient, the danger is that he will fall "in love" with therapy, lending himself too completely to an all-enveloping and seductive process. I am not suggesting that significant changes can take place without the patient sometimes feeling engulfed by the experience. But it is most inappropriate when a person is so "in love" with therapy that he sees it as a new religion and his treatment as a salvation.

There is also a danger for the psychotherapist that he may come to see his way of solving people's problems as the best, or even the *only* way. This too is "religious" in its approach, and has often led to the exclusivity claimed by various groups of therapists. Psychotherapy is not the exclusive domain of any one group, with all others to be considered interlopers.

There is another attitude about psychotherapy with respect to which my view has changed markedly over the years. During my training I was told that undesirable behavior was a result of inner conflict, and that valid insight therapies concerned themselves only with the causes and not with the behavior itself. I was taught that to be judgmental about any form of behavior on the patient's part would be wrong for a therapist. This is entirely incorrect.

A therapist must somehow deal with destructive, constricting, or self-defeating behavior. He must stand on the side of constructive and effective living on the part of the patient. To say that the therapist must not reveal his position on such matters is foolish. Can the therapist not address the fact that the patient is depressed, or suicidal, or homicidal, or a thief, or a hermit? Can he avoid letting his feelings be known about the patient's use of drugs or repeated involvement with destructive partners? Of course not. A sine qua non of psychotherapy is that the therapist stand for what is right and best for both the patient and for society: it is impossible for the therapist not to take a stand. In all therapies, including psychoanalysis, the therapist will be for some things and against others. The excessively or deceptively passive therapist may choose not to show such leanings, but, nonetheless, many of them will be known to the patient. When a noninterventionist position is taken too far, endless therapy can occur without effect; many of the failures of psychotherapy can be attributed to the fact that therapists have worked in this misguided way.

Bob has been my friend for many years. He has an infectious warmth, and is broadly liked because of his sense of humor. He lives with much pleasure, and travels a great deal. He is a highly social person.

Bob has never been treated in psychotherapy. He has had occasion to meet numerous psychiatrists and analysts. He has had close friends who have been in treatment, a few who have found their treatment satisfactory, some who have not. One day we talked about some aspects of this work, and that, he felt, something was missing from the therapists he had met.

"I know," he suddenly exclaimed, "I know what is wrong. They have absolutely no sense of humor. They are unresponsive, and cannot see what is funny in life. How could they help other people find pleasure in living?"

Bob had made an important observation. In discussing some of the problems that I have come to see as most important for psychotherapy, I do not want to convey the view that it is a subject about which one should only be serious. It is true that psychotherapy with unhappy and disturbed patients has much pain and pressure for both patient and therapist. It is hard work, yet when the warm and humorous side of life emerges within the treatment there is much good feeling in the process. We analysts have to be taught that although we do serious work we must not take ourselves too seriously. There is an important place for humor in psychotherapy.

With Zelda, my first psychoanalytic patient, two principal issues needed to be dealt with in the course of our work together. One was her feelings about being a woman. The other was her conviction that there was something wrong or unattractive about her body, a feeling which largely related to her back. It was obvious that these two problems were connected psychologically, and many of these connections, some of which were sexual, became clear in the analytic work.

Zelda's treatment lasted for three years. After that I would see her about once a year, and she would bring me up to date on the developments in her life. After one such visit, when I told her that I was very interested in understanding what had helped her in the analysis, she sent me several poems, the following two of which are relevant to our present topic.

> "After spending three years in analysis,
> And growing posterior callouses,
> I've begun to be me
> And have started to see
> That two boobs are as good as a phallus is."

> "For analysis I'll always vouch,
> It reduced my 'hunch back' to a slouch.
> Was this due to lost fears?
> Or simply the years
> I lay flat on my back on the couch?"

The analysis was hard work for both Zelda and myself. But it was filled with considerable good humor and much satisfaction. Her poems illustrate her attitude to the undertaking: it was worthwhile and to be respected, but entirely worthy of some good fun. The attitude did much to sustain us during the most trying times of the analysis.

A clear distinction must be made between humor which is experienced as helpful and pleasurable to the patient, and humor which feels to him unwanted and destructive. Seriously depressed patients will not be cheered by humor, they will be made to feel more desolate and not understood. Schizophrenic patients, especially when paranoid suspicions prevail, are highly likely to misinterpret any lightheartedness as being aimed at mocking them or laughing at them. On the other hand, some severely disturbed patients are able to be shown the ludicrousness of their thoughts, or even their delusions, and the use of humor may make them begin to question some of their ideas.

The practice of psychotherapy requires freedom. This includes the freedom as a person to be natural and spontaneous and emotional, the freedom to be angry and even to hate the patient, and most important, the freedom to care for and even to love the patient. When such freedom does not exist in the therapist, the results of the treatment will be severely limited. There is much to be learned in training. Unfortunately, facts and theories often stand in the way of that personal freedom and spontaneity which make for effective work.

I have experienced a difficult conflict within myself which I believe many psychotherapists face: on the one hand, with the conservatism and scepticism which are encouraged in both college and medical school, there is the tendency to approach the work from the academic point of view so as to avoid violating established scientific principles; on the other hand, there is the instinctive urge toward closeness with others which stems from one's natural human warmth and spontaneity. I have tried to bring these two together in a scientific and emotionally valid amalgam.

At this stage of my life and my work, I often find myself speaking for more freedom of action than journal articles, conferences, and many psychotherapy texts prescribe. The reason for this is that I have found that my most successful work with patients has resulted when I have increasingly been myself. The freedom to be oneself in a very similar way in all circumstances—in the consulting room or elsewhere in one's own life—is a freedom of great significance. In fact, it is one of the cardinal goals which should be sought by and for the patient in therapy.

Having gained the capacity to explore freely, I find the therapeutic work most stimulating and exciting. It is a tremendous frustration for a psychotherapist when he feels bound and inhibited. Freedom of action gives the work vitality. As a result, I find that in recent years my work in therapy feels increasingly creative. More and more options appear, both within the work and within my own life. This is entirely in keeping with what I encourage and seek for my patients within their lives.

I do not know of more interesting work that a person can do. Every time I begin with a new patient I feel myself privileged to enter into a new world. There is always the unknown as one begins. The entire course of the therapy aims at eliminating as much of that unknown, for both the participants, as possible. Because of the patient's hurts and scars many barriers have been erected. The work is not easy, as his vulnerability and self-protectiveness must be taken into account when trying to achieve understanding. Yet every time, as the work progresses, there is the excitement of each new discovery, as well as the pleasure of becoming close to another worthwhile human being.

I like the work because one can never become a master of it. The more accomplished one is, the more effortless one's function as a therapist becomes, the more there still remains to be clarified and understood. Because the challenge of becoming trusted to the fullest possible degree by someone else is so great, one is always on one's mettle. This is not a profession which becomes automatic in the practice, and so I find that I never become bored with it. One certainly becomes tired, but not bored, and not uninterested. The more I learn about others, the more I continue to learn about myself. I do not feel fixed in my ideas, but rather see continual opportunities for change and growth. This gives me a sense of freshness and vigor in the work and, in a parallel way, in my life. Having options for change is something that the profession of psychotherapy as a whole requires so that it can make appropriate alterations and developments and will not stultify.

My greatest satisfaction has been that of seeing sick people become well, and stunted and inhibited people grow and develop. It has been most rewarding to see how those valuable people, freed to be themselves, could create so much and affect so many others in positive ways. My next greatest satisfaction has been that of learning so much about people and about the world from those who have agreed to share their worlds with me. And my final great satisfaction has been that wonderful by-product of the work: the friends I have made. From the ranks of my patients have come some of the most intensely satisfying friendships that I have known. In those instances when a great like-mindedness has been recognized during the work, the growth of the patient has led, eventually, to an end of the therapeutic working relation per se. But what has persisted has been a warm, caring, informed, and loving friendship, which has given me tremendous satisfaction, filling me with gratitude for the meaning of my work.

I have arrived at the conclusion that psychotherapy is not a set of rules about what one should and should not do. I have tried in this book to put forward my view of what psychotherapy is. It is very complex, and yet it is simple. It is the meeting and working together of two people; it is hard honest work.

You might say, it is a labor of love.

BIBLIOGRAPHY

Baum, L. Frank. *The Wizard of Oz*. London: Hutchinson & Co., 1939.

Frank, Jerome D. *Persuasion and Healing: A Comparative Study of Psychotherapy*. Baltimore, MD: The Johns Hopkins Press, 1961.

Fromm-Reichmann, Frieda. *Psychoanalysis and Psychotherapy*. Edited by Dexter M. Bullard. Chicago, IL: University of Chicago Press, 1959.

Greben, Stanley E. "Some Difficulties and Satisfactions Inherent in the Practice of Psychoanalysis." *International Journal of Psycho-Analysis 56* (1975): 427–434.

———. "The Essence of Psychotherapy." *British Journal of Psychiatry 138* (1981): 449–455.

———. "Unresponsiveness: The Demon Artefact of Psychotherapy." *American Journal of Psychotherapy 35* (1981): 244–250.

———. "Some Sources of Conflict within Psychoanalytic Societies." *International Journal of Psychoanalytic Psychotherapy 9* (1982): 201–209.

———. "Bad Theater in Psychotherapy: The Case for Therapists' Liberation." *American Journal of Psychotherapy 37* (1983): 69–76.

Green, Hannah. "In Praise of My Doctor—Frieda [Fromm-]Reichmann." *Contemporary Psychoanalysis 4* (1967): 7[

Greenson, Ralph R. *The Technique and Practice of Psy[choanalysis*.] New York: International Universities Press, 196[

Horton, Paul C. *Solace: The Missing Dimension [in Psychiatry*.] Chicago, IL: University of Chicago Press, 198[

Lampl-de Groot, Jeanne. "Personal Experien[ces with Psycho]analytic Technique and Theory during th[e last Half Cen]tury." *Psychoanalytic Study of the Child 31* [(1976): ___.] New Haven, CT: Yale University Press[

Thomas, Alexander, and Chess, Stella. [*Temperament and De]velopment*. New York: Brunner/Mazel[